The White House in Gingerbread

Memories & Recipes

The WHITE HOUSE IN GINGERBREAD

Memories & Recipes

ROLAND MESNIER
WITH MARK RAMSDELL

Forewords by Rosalynn Carter and Laura Bush

WHITE HOUSE HISTORICAL ASSOCIATION

WASHINGTON, D.C.

The WHITE HOUSE HISTORICAL ASSOCIATION is a nonprofit organization, chartered on November 3, 1961, to enhance understanding, appreciation, and enjoyment of the historic White House. Income from the sale of the association's books and guides is returned to the publications program and is used as well to acquire historical furnishings and memorabilia for the White House.

This book has been brought to publication through the generous assistance of the Hon. Walter H. Annenberg White House Publications Fund.

VICE PRESIDENT OF PUBLISHING AND EXECUTIVE EDITOR: Marcia Mallet Anderson
EDITORIAL DIRECTOR: Fiona Griffin
PRODUCTION MANAGER: Lauren A. Zook
EDITORIAL SPECIALIST: Rhonda Murchison
CONSULTING EDITOR: Ann Hofstra Grogg

First Edition
10 9 8 7 6 5 4 3 2 1
Library of Congress Control Number: 2015940935
ISBN 978-1-931917-47-6
Printed in Italy

This book is for all the young up-and-coming pastry chefs in the world. May it inspire you to be the best you can be. Remember the road to success is paved with experience. I had half a century of fun. So will you. Be honest, hard working, dedicated, and humble. Bless you all! — Roland Mesnier

To my wife Sue and my children Matthew and Amanda for their loving, patient, and constant support of my pastry career; and to my grandchildren Andrew and Caroline for helping me to appreciate the joy of gingerbread houses through the eyes of children. — Mark Ramsdell

CONTENTS

MEMORIES OF THE WHITE HOUSE IN GINGERBREAD

MAKING YOUR OWN GINGERBREAD HOUSE

WHITE HOUSE HOLIDAY RECIPES

FOREWORD

I FIRST MET ROLAND MESNIER IN 1979 WHEN HE CAME TO INTERVIEW FOR THE POSITION OF PASTRY CHEF IN THE WHITE HOUSE KITCHEN. It was a challenging and high-pressure position, but Chef Mesnier took it on with extraordinary enthusiasm and dedication. From the very beginning he was constantly creating new recipes, and he would often personalize desserts for our guests according to their tastes and interests.

One of the most memorable desserts Chef Mesnier created for us was the cake for Jimmy's birthday on October 1, 1980, which was decorated with a blown-sugar donkey. I also remember the chocolate creations that he made for Amy at Easter, and I know she enjoyed baking her own cookies after school in his Pastry Shop.

Among Chef Mesnier's extraordinary desserts for our official guests was a lovely orange sherbet génoise—prepared entirely with kosher ingredients—for Prime Minister Menachem Begin of Israel. And for a luncheon in honor of His Majesty King Baudouin of Belgium he served an unusual coconut ice cream presented in delicate hibiscus flower shells of pulled sugar.

Chef Mesnier's stories of creating the White House gingerbread houses, holiday cookies, and special desserts bring back wonderful memories of the holiday season at the White House. Christmas was a special time for our family, and we enjoyed welcoming many hundreds of guests to celebrate with us. Chef Mesnier worked hard to ensure that every detail, down to the last cookie, made their visit a once-in-a-lifetime experience.

I hope this book will give you a sense of what the festive season was like during Chef Mesnier's tenure at the White House—and that it will encourage you to build your own gingerbread house!

Rosalynn Carter

The birthday cake Chef Mesnier made for President Carter's birthday at the height of the 1980 presidential campaign (*above*) was decorated—appropriately—with a blown-sugar donkey.

On a return visit to the White House in 1989 (*opposite*), former First Lady Rosalynn Carter is greeted by Chef Mesnier, whom she had hired a decade earlier.

FOREWORD

EVERY DECEMBER WHEN GEORGE AND I LIVED AT THE WHITE HOUSE I COULDN'T WAIT TO SEE THE GINGERBREAD HOUSE, the centerpiece of the White House Christmas decorations. The White House gingerbread house is an architectural and engineering marvel, requiring perfectly baked walls and meticulous assembly, using just the right amount of sticky, sweet mortar. A tradition begun by First Lady Pat Nixon in 1972, the annual gingerbread house has grown from a quaint gumdrop and candy-cane decorated chalet into exacting replicas of iconic homes from American and presidential history.

Executive Pastry Chef Roland Mesnier unveiled a beautifully decorated gingerbread house in 2001 when our Christmas theme was "Home for the Holidays," and the decorations featured the homes of many of our presidents. Chef Mesnier had built a detailed gingerbread replica of the White House as it appeared when President John Adams was in residence. President Adams was the first president to live in the White House.

Then to fulfill our theme of "All Creatures Great and Small in the White House" in 2002, Chef Mesnier used eighty pounds of gingerbread and fifty pounds of chocolate to build the gingerbread White House. And he stirred up some twenty pounds of marzipan to sculpt the sweet likeness of the many beloved pets that have belonged to our presidents and their families. For "A Season of Stories" in 2003, classic children's books and stories set the scene for the gingerbread White House. Humpty Dumpty sat on the White House balcony, and the Cat in the Hat danced by the front door with a candy cane.

Chef Mesnier and the White House Historical Association have come together to share this wonderful holiday tradition with everyone. *The White House in Gingerbread* includes tempting recipes and gingerbread house–building tips with the chef's personal stories of building gingerbread houses. The sale of the books supports the White House Historical Association's important work to preserve and conserve the White House public rooms for all Americans to enjoy.

Here's to a sweet holiday season!

Laura Bush

First Lady Laura Bush bids farewell to Chef Mesnier on his retirement in 2004 (*above*).

Chef Mesnier unveiled the Home for the Holidays gingerbread White House for the Bushes first Christmas in the White House in 2001.

PREFACE

My MEMORIES TRANSPORT ME BACK TO A TIME, JUST A FEW YEARS AGO AND A FEW DAYS BEFORE CHRISTMAS, when I was the White House executive pastry chef and the annual White House holiday parties have come to an end. We are busily cleaning the Pastry Shop. This is the time of year we go through everything—every refrigerator, walk-in cooler, freezer, and cabinet. Leftover cookies, cakes, and chocolate will be given to the White House staff as a way to say "thank you" for working so hard to make the holiday events a success and to make the holidays a little sweeter for their families who have not seen much of them since Thanksgiving. After a short break, we will get back to work planning the next events of the new year. As always, Christmas will consume a big part of the Pastry Shop's time in the coming year. We will go through a list of all the things that need to be addressed, changed, or improved upon. I will even begin planning for next Christmas by reviewing the dessert menu and considering new desserts and decorations for trays and tables.

My memories now take me to a June day when it is time for holiday baking to start. We gather all the ingredients—the nuts and the dried, candied, and macerated fruits necessary to bake a half ton of fruit cakes. We will begin baking fruit cakes soon, even though it is early summer. The finished cakes will be refrigerated—the longer the better for the flavor to mature. Although the holiday baking is officially under way, it must be timed to accommodate the constant flow of official, ceremonial, and private events such as State Dinners, receptions, and first family gatherings. As the weeks go by, we will ease into making and shaping the many varieties of cookies that will be frozen and then baked fresh throughout the holiday season. We start with macaroons, leckerlis, and Florentines. While we attend to the daily entertaining requirements of the house, we cannot ignore the fact that we are getting closer to the holidays. The Pastry Kitchen is small, so we need to be working from a perfect master plan to accommodate the amount of work required. We must constantly be aware of the need to produce more and more desserts. As we get closer to the holidays we start baking and freezing sheet pans lined with pâte sucrée, sponge cakes, and roulade biscuits for the buche de Noel as well as rings of banana, carrot, and pumpkin cakes. We will make gallons of ganache, mousse, buttercream, and

Holiday baking in the White House Pastry kitchen was usually officially under way by June of each year. Several months were spent preparing thousands of cookies and hundreds of edible decorations. In the scene captured in a photograph taken in the White House kitchen in 1992, Chef Mesnier is sprinkling powdered sugar on the American Village Gingerbread house, while assistant Marlene Roudebush forms a marzipan Santa Claus.

By November of each year, Chef Mesnier and his Pastry Shop staff would set up a temporary work space in the White House China Room, where they would construct the annual gingerbread house. Work continued nonstop until about Thanksgiving, when the Operations Crew would move the completed showpiece to the State Dining Room for display throughout the holidays.

bavarians that are needed to fill and glaze the cakes, and many different flavors of buche de Noel with endless marzipan decorations. During these early months of holiday preparations, the Pastry Shop remains ready to bake for all events on the White House agenda. As we get closer to the holidays we will start baking stollen, panettone, savarin rings, and, last but not least, the twenty-five to thirty full sheet pans of gingerbread needed for constructing the annual showpiece. By now my Pastry Shop assistants have been working for several months to make hundreds of edible decorations out of marzipan, pastillage, royal icing, and chocolate.

And now I am seeing the beginning of November. Things are shifting into high gear. I am hiring part-time workers to help with the increasing work load. This is the time of the year when I concentrate my energy on the special gingerbread house—a project anticipated throughout the White House. The plans for the house have been brought together and adjustments made on the design until the first lady approves. Now we are ready to build, and our temporary work space is set up in the China Room on the Ground Floor of the White House near the kitchen. The floors and furniture are protected with plastic sheeting, and long worktables are brought in along with the tools needed to create the large-scale gingerbread house—a large band saw, measuring and cutting instruments, a commercial mixer, a personal pastry toolbox, and several chocolate warmers. Construction continues nonstop until about Thanksgiving,

The White House gingerbread house and holiday decorations are traditionally unveiled at a press preview like the one seen here in 2006. The first lady and the many members of the White House staff who have prepared the decorations are present to answer questions.

when the Operations Crew safely moves the finished gingerbread house to the State Dining Room. Once the gingerbread house is set up, we are now ready for visitors. The first event of the season is the press preview. Here the first lady unveils the Christmas decorations and the gingerbread house to everyone. The Flower Shop, Electric Shop, carpenters, and plumbers at the White House do a superb job. They are a talented group of dedicated professionals. The first lady leads the press on a tour through the White House and takes questions about the decorations. Afterward there will be a party for the press preview and the amount of food and drink guests consume is over the top. My calculations for the Pastry Shop were accurate—at least five pieces of cake or cookies per person. In reality, during the three holiday weeks we will serve about 35,000 guests.

Today I am retired, and it is pleasure to share my memories and recipes from the twenty-five years I spent at the White House. Chef Mark Ramsdell and I hope your White House invitation will soon be in the mail for the holiday, but in case it does not arrive, we hope you will enjoy the White House Christmas through this book.

Roland Mesnier
July 2015

GINGERBREAD FOR THE PRESIDENT
A TRADITION BEGINS

Chef Hans Raffert puts the finishing touches on the German A-frame ginger-bread house in 1981 in the State Dining Room.

A Tradition Begins

THE FIRST WHITE HOUSE GINGERBREAD HOUSE was built by Assistant Executive Chef Hans Raffert in 1969 for First Lady Patricia Nixon. This began a tradition that he continued through 1991, when he built his last White House gingerbread house for President George H. W. Bush. Chef Raffert's houses were all variations on the traditional German A-frame design and featured versions of the story of Hansel and Gretel. Over the years, his houses grew bigger and more ornate, incorporating many pounds of colorful jelly beans, assorted hard candies, and candy canes. Chef Raffert's creations became a popular signature of the holiday celebrations in the State Dining Room.

First Lady Patricia Nixon presents one of the early gingerbread houses made for the White House and displayed prominently in the State Dining Room, 1972. The press covering the story are seen reflected in the mirror.

Chef Raffert made his traditional German A-frame gingerbread houses during President Gerald R. Ford's administration. Clockwise from top left: Hansel and Gretel approach the door of a candy-covered house displayed in the State Dining Room; First Lady Betty Ford decorates cookies with daughter Susan; and, when President and Mrs. Ford returned to the White House in 2003, during the George H. W. Bush administration, Chef Roland Mesnier made a special cake, elaborately decorated with blown-sugar ribbons, to celebrate the former president's 90th birthday.

During the administration of President Jimmy Carter, Chef Raffert continued to make gingerbread houses in the A-frame style. The president's daughter Amy (*above*) views a house embellished with candy canes, gingerbread men, and reindeer. President and Mrs. Carter pose with Amy (*right*), in front of the Blue Room Christmas tree, 1978.

First Lady Nancy Reagan was delighted by Chef Raffert's house that incorporated President Reagan's favorite candy—jelly beans—in 1984. Below, she reviews the plans for a holiday buffet. The first trays of cookies and sweets prepared by Chef Mesnier's Pastry Shop are placed on the table in the State Dining Room.

NEW BEGINNINGS

A CHRISTMAS VILLAGE

In 1992 during the George H. W.
Bush administration, Chef Roland
Mesnier, pictured here with First Lady
Barbara Bush, was selected to take
over the construction of the annual
White House gingerbread showpiece.
For the next twelve years, Chef Mes-
nier and his staff built gingerbread
houses of many designs.

THE AMERICAN CHRISTMAS VILLAGE

PRESIDENT GEORGE H. W. BUSH AND FIRST LADY BARBARA BUSH enjoyed celebrating Christmas with their large family, which included five children and a growing number of grandchildren. During the holidays, the family spent time together at Camp David. President Bush could be found reading Christmas stories to his grandchildren and listening to the Marine carolers at Evergreen Chapel. First Lady Barbara Bush later reminisced that their grandchildren helped keep the holiday spirit alive.

At the White House, the first lady helped facilitate the decorations and holiday themes. Although I was hired as executive pastry chef in 1979, it wasn't until 1992 that I oversaw the construction of the annual gingerbread house. For my first house, Mrs. Bush gave me permission to be as creative as I wanted to be and so I undertook the construction of an entire gingerbread village, which consisted of five separate gingerbread houses.

First Lady Barbara Bush played Santa's helper with her grandchildren at the White House in 1991. In Chef Mesnier's American Christmas Village, Mrs. Bush was portrayed in marzipan carrying a tray of cookies to her grandchildren.

WHEN I DESIGNED THE DECORATIONS FOR THE AMERICAN CHRISTMAS VILLAGE, I worked to create personal touches that would especially delight the president and first lady's grandchildren. My gingerbread creation included marzipan likenesses of the first family interspersed among the sledding elves, frolicking reindeer, and Santa Claus posing in a rocking chair. A light dusting of powdered sugar snow completed the picturesque scene.

WHILE WORKING IN THE WHITE HOUSE, I could never anticipate what special requests would come my way, and this was particularly true during the holidays. On one occasion the Bushes had just finished dinner with a small group of friends and I was in my office getting ready to go home when Mrs. Bush called me to the State Dining Room. I had no idea what this was all about. It turned out she wanted me to talk to her guests about the American Christmas Village and explain how it was constructed. She was so pleased with my presentation that she invited me to join a Christmas sing-along. I soon realized that Neil Diamond was at the piano with Julie Andrews! I never felt so uncomfortable in my life because I might be the worst singer in the world. I prayed that the floor would open and I would fall through. I believe that because Mr. Diamond recognized my plight he told Mrs. Bush he did not have the appropriate sheet music to continue. The party ended, and I was off the hook. I was so grateful.

In December 1992 Neil Diamond and Julie Andrews performed at the National Building Museum in Washington, D.C., for the "Christmas in Washington" program *(opposite)*. At the end of the program, the president and Mrs. Bush joined the choir in singing Christmas carols.

My talented pastry assistant Marlene Roudebush began work at the White House in 1992. She continued to prepare marzipan decorations for all of my gingerbread projects over the years and must have shaped thousands of pounds of marzipan—ultimately earning the title of "Marzipan Queen."

FOR THE CHRISTMAS VILLAGE, as with all of the houses we built over the years, advanced preparation of hundreds of details was required. The preparation of all the marzipan and sugar decorations began as soon as the theme was selected—well before the house itself was built. This process involved many hours of work and was completed on days when the president traveled and the pastry staff had more time to focus on the winter holidays that loomed ahead.

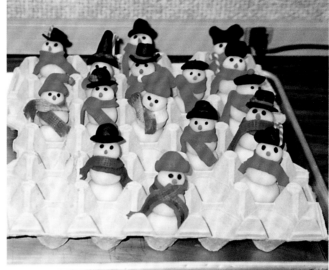

Chef Mesnier's White House Pastry Shop produced marzipan figures by the hundreds each Christmas. Seen here are trays of Santas, teddy bears, and snowmen ready and waiting to be positioned in the gingerbread scene.

WELCOMING A NEW FIRST FAMILY
THE HOUSE OF SOCKS

President William Jefferson Clinton was inaugurated in January 1993. For the Clintons' first Christmas in the White House, Chef Mesnier chose to honor their celebrity cat with the House of Socks Gingerbread House. Here, President and Mrs. Clinton view the gingerbread house in the State Dining Room.

THE HOUSE OF SOCKS

WITH THE 1993 INAUGURATION OF A NEW PRESIDENT of the United States came the arrival of William J. Clinton, his wife Hillary Clinton, and their 12-year-old daughter Chelsea to the White House. As with every new first family, we had to learn and adapt to their habits and tastes. For the Clintons' first Christmas at the White House, I decided to create a gingerbread house that would make their family feel welcome, and so I made the House of Socks as a tribute to their family cat named Socks, a black and white former stray.

The House of Socks remains one of my favorite gingerbread house projects because it was a perfect replica built from plans that were drawn to scale. Gold curtains were rolled out of fondant and attached in different positions on the inside of every window, just as if wind were blowing through the rooms. The windows were finished with dried royal icing pieces, which had been carefully piped to show the architectural detail of the window casings and mullions. Various sizes and shapes of trees, piped in chocolate and covered with green sugar sprinkles, were placed all around the exterior of the house. Miniature working electric spotlights were positioned in front of the House of Socks to show off the details of the building.

Socks was a favorite of the press. Even while the Clintons were still living in Little Rock, Arkansas, press photographers would surround Socks wherever he went. At the White House, Socks made himself at home. The Secret Service often took him on walks around the house and the grounds. He even once appeared for a photo-op at the podium in the press briefing room. Socks enjoyed the gingerbread house made in his honor during Christmas so much that he decided to taste it!

After the baking for the House of Socks was complete, the gingerbread house was assembled in the White House China Room in front of television cameras. Here Chef Mesnier is using tempered couverture chocolate to join the walls together. When finished, the house featured twenty-two marzipan sculptures of Socks. It weighed nearly 100 pounds and took 150 hours to build.

In 1993, Mark Ramsdell joined my pastry team at the White House and incorporated innovation and creativity in each of the houses he worked on. Ramsdell also served as director and head instructor of the Pastry Arts Program at L'Academie de Cuisine, a culinary program established in 1980. Many of his students went on to became part-time staff for the White House.

Surprises for the President and First Lady
Two Childhood Homes

THE PRESIDENT'S BOYHOOD HOME

IN 1994 WE DECIDED TO SURPRISE PRESIDENT CLINTON by replicating a house that was personal to him—his boyhood home in Hot Springs, Arkansas, where he lived from 1954 to 1961. We were fortunate to have advice from Carolyn Huber, who worked for the Clintons as an aide beginning in 1983 at the Arkansas Governor's Mansion and later at the White House. She provided pictures that enabled us to accurately reproduce the distinctive half-timbered, Tudor-style house with the curved roofline on the front. The project was kept a complete secret until the day it was unveiled. The president was very appreciative of our efforts, and I am sure I saw a tear in his eye when he saw the gingerbread house was actually his home.

THE PRESIDENT'S BOYHOOD HOME PROJECT PRESENTED MANY CHALLENGES, but the details—such as the green royal icing floodwork on the exposed structural timbers—made the house immediately recognizable, particularly to the president himself. A marzipan model of a dog eagerly waits on the front porch, and a freshly baked pie sits on the window sill. To add the spirit of Christmas, Santa Claus sits on the roof while his reindeer stand with a marzipan snowman on the front lawn.

I remember that the Clintons' favorite holiday centerpieces were blown-sugar snowmen. I used these sugar snowmen on cookie trays or grouped them together into Christmas scenes and displayed them on the table. The three sections of the snowman were blown separately and glued together with hot sugar.

THE FIRST LADY'S CHILDHOOD HOME

IN 1995 WE DECIDED TO HONOR MRS. CLINTON by making a copy of her childhood home on North Wisner Street in Park Ridge, Illinois. Carolyn Huber once again supplied pictures of the house for reference so we could capture such details as the molding on the front door, the distinctive window design, and the profusion of ivy climbing up the front wall. For the first time, we exposed interior spaces by opening sections of the exterior wall. I revealed a child's bedroom and the living room in the house in order to illustrate two scenes set on the night before Christmas.

IN THE TWO EXPOSED ROOMS, I RE-CREATED SCENES FROM THE POEM "'TWAS THE NIGHT BEFORE CHRISTMAS." The girl's bedroom depicted the line "While visions of sugar-plums danced in their heads" with a portrayal of the first lady as a sleeping child whose dream of sugarplums appears on her bedroom wall. We placed a trunk at the foot of the bed and a dresser—complete with an electrified marzipan lamp—against the sidewall. In the living room, set in the right side of the gingerbread house, we created the scene "The stockings were hung by the chimney with care" with a marzipan rug, a working floor lamp, and a fully decorated Christmas tree beside the chimney hung with stockings. The ivy crawling up the front of the house was made with individually fashioned leaves. We used multiple shades of green royal icing to achieve realistic depth and shading.

First Lady Hillary Clinton presents the 1995 official Blue Room Christmas tree *(top)*. This 18½-foot Fraser fir was decorated with building-themed ornaments such as rooftops, shutters, and chimneys were made by the American Institute of Architecture students.

Chef Mesnier posed with Chef Susie Morrison in 1995 *(right)* during the construction of the First Lady's Childhood Home Gingerbread House.

Mrs. CLINTON'S CHILDHOOD HOME WAS DESIGNED IN KEEPING WITH THE BROADER 1995 WHITE HOUSE HOLIDAY THEME, which was inspired by the popular poem "A Visit From St. Nicholas," written by Clement C. Moore in 1823. For many families—even the first family—reading this poem aloud on Christmas Eve is one of the season's treasured rituals. All throughout the White House, reminders of this poem could be found. The many elements of the house inspired by the poem included a herd of Santa's Reindeer that we placed on the lawn. The completed house weighed 70 pounds.

Following my retirement, Chef Morrison continued to work in the White House Pastry Shop as the assistant pastry chef and in 2014 she became the executive pastry chef—the first woman to hold this position at the White House.

In 2010 Susie Morrison worked on a molded white chocolate replica of the White House (*left*). The Obamas' dog Bo stands guard by the South Portico.

CHELSEA'S TURN

THE NUTCRACKER

THE NUTCRACKER

AFTER HONORING THE FAMILY CAT and then the President and Mrs. Clinton with the first three houses of the Clinton administration, we decided that 1996 would be Chelsea Clinton's turn. We decided to bring to life the story of *The Nutcracker*, a ballet that she danced with the Washington Ballet group in Washington, D.C.

We created all of the characters from *The Nutcracker* with icing, and they filled the large central room posed in motion. The figure in the front right, dressed in a pink dress, is a likeness of Chelsea attending her own Christmas party. The ever-present Socks appeared in a painting hung on the back wall. I placed two large gingerbread nutcrackers as guards on the front steps. They were colorfully painted in icing sugar. Another reminder of Christmas was Santa Claus arriving in a sleigh pulled by reindeer. This gingerbread house was yet again completed in total secrecy, and Chelsea was touched by our efforts. She immediately found herself in the pink dress and was very pleased.

Bill Clinton holds Chelsea (on the left) after one of her earliest dance recitals *(top)* at the Children's House Montessori School. In 1996 she performed in *The Nutcracker* with the Washington Ballet *(above)*.

THE FIRST BALLET PERFORMANCE CHELSEA CLINTON attended was none other than Pyotr Ilich Tchaikovsky's *The Nutcracker.* The ballet tells the story of Clara, a young girl who saves the Nutcracker Prince from the Mouse King and escapes on a dream adventure through the Land of Sweets. At the age of two, Chelsea gave her first ballet performance in Little Rock, Arkansas, and she continued to dance as she grew up—most often in productions of *The Nutcracker.*

While living in Washington, D.C., Chelsea remained a *Nutcracker* dancer with

the Washington School of Ballet. On December 8, 1993, she performed the role of the Favorite Aunt. In 1996, at the age of 16, Chelsea took on several roles in the Washington Ballet's annual production and had fourteen performances scheduled. *The Nutcracker* enthralled not only Chelsea Clinton but also her parents, and the ballet became a highlight of their Christmases throughout the years.

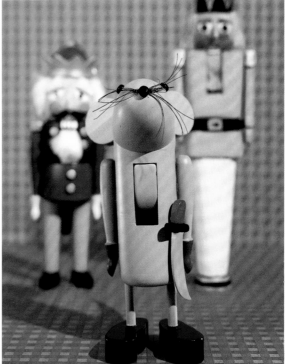

In 1996, *The Nutcracker* was the theme not only for the White House gingerbread house but also for all of the White House holiday decorations. The decorations and ornaments for trees throughout the house were created by three artistic groups—ballet companies, woodworking artists, and the American Needlepoint and Embroiderer's Guilds. Examples of their work included an ornament featuring Clara holding the Nutcracker Prince *(opposite)*, knit stockings embroidered with scenes from the ballet *(left)*, and a handmade wooden Mouse King *(above)*.

THE NORTH POLE
SANTA'S WORKSHOP

I never knew what was going to be popular, but in 1997 it was Santa's cell phone that got the most attention. Nestled in his sleigh, Santa was prepared to leave to distribute gifts to children around the world. But this Christmas he was equipped with the latest technology. In his hand, Santa held a cell phone so he would be ready to receive last-minute requests. The members of the press were thrilled with the phone. It was all they could talk about.

THE WHITE HOUSE IN GINGERBREAD

A work in progress: the walls and roof of Santa's Workshop Gingerbread House were assembled in the China Room *(right),* and a tray held a collection of marzipan toys, ready for placement to complete the scene *(below).*

1997: SANTA'S WORKSHOP

Marlene Roudebush, the "Marzipan Queen," was in her element during this project, making hundreds of marzipan figures and toys. The exposed front of Santa's Workshop captured the busiest time of the year at the North Pole—the Christmas season. The workshop was filled with marzipan elves building toys of all kinds. Their tools, plans, materials, and Santa's "Naughty or Nice" list were spread out across the floor. We even hung Santa's spare red suit on the wall.

A FAIRY TALE WINTER

THE WONDERLAND CASTLE

THE WONDERLAND CASTLE

THE OVERALL THEME FOR THE WHITE HOUSE DECORATIONS in 1998 was a "Winter Wonderland." I decided that my contribution would be a Wonderland Castle made of gingerbread—a perfect centerpiece for the State Dining Room. I envisioned something that would capture the essence of a classic fairy tale. With childlike abandon, I let my imagination, and the project, take me wherever it would go, and I created the castle in its entirety without plans. The result was huge—my biggest house ever. With a 4 x 8 foot base, the castle could be placed only on the long State Dining Room table instead of in its usual place on a side table against the wall. The table is usually reserved for the savory food, but this year it was used for the pastries. We filled it with an endless stream of festive Christmas sweets (many of which are described elsewhere in this book). The castle was set on an even larger base decorated with royal icing to appear as if it were resting atop rock cliffs high in the mountains.

The magnitude of this particular gingerbread house created an unusual amount of stress. Moving a project of this size was my biggest concern. The press was always present when the gingerbread house was moved from our Pastry Shop into the State Dining Room, and an accident would make the perfect photo opportunity. As the Operations Crew was moving the castle from cart to table, one of the towers began to topple over. Thankfully my guardian angel was on duty that day. The tiny electric lights and wires secured with chocolate to the castle stopped the collapse. The wires held the tower at a 45-degree angle. Using one finger, I calmly lifted the tower back upright and acknowledged the applause from the press. A close call to be sure.

I remember that President and Mrs. Clinton loved the figures of the president's dog Buddy and their cat Socks ice skating on a frozen pond. They were made of cast sugar and royal icing and placed beside the castle, which was set on a forested mountain.

A drop door between the two large towers provided an exit for Santa and his sleigh.

MILLENNIUM CELEBRATION

Treasures of the Nation's Capital

TREASURES OF THE NATION'S CAPITAL

I USUALLY HELPED WITH THE SELECTION OF THE HOLIDAY DECORATION THEME and the concept for the gingerbread house. But the Christmas of 1999 was extraordinary—the last Christmas of the century. As we looked toward the new millennium, President and Mrs. Clinton wanted to honor the past. Americans from across the country were invited to decorate the White House with representations of national landmarks and portraits of those who helped shape our country. The first lady announced she wanted the gingerbread display to include a collection of houses—the architectural treasures of the nation's capital.

The first would be the White House—a major project in itself. In addition, the presentation would include the Washington Monument, complete with its blinking red lights; the Jefferson Memorial; Mount Vernon; and the Potomac River meandering through the display. Mrs. Clinton's decision was announced in early November, so the pressure was on to build quickly! We had four substantial gingerbread houses to prepare in less time than we usually spent making one.

In 1999 the gingerbread buildings remained on display until after the New Year. For the millennium celebration Chef Mesnier added marzipan swags and fruit topiaries, traditional colonial Christmas decorations, and sugar fireworks to the tops of the four gingerbread buildings.

Our work on the land-
marks collection of
gingerbread houses
was done in conjunction
with preparations for
the millennium celebra-
tions to be held at
the White House on
December 31, 1999. The
festivities began with a
sit-down dinner for 700
people at 7 p.m. After
dinner the President and
Mrs. Clinton went to
the National Mall to
participate in "America's
Millennium: A Celebra-
tion for the Nation."
They then returned to
the White House, where
a midnight buffet had
been prepared for 1,600
guests. After a night of
revelry, we prepared a
breakfast buffet for
600 guests the next
morning. That was a very
busy day that went on
for twenty-four hours
nonstop.

CHRISTMASES OF THE CLINTON WHITE HOUSE

CHRISTMASES OF THE CLINTON WHITE HOUSE

IN 2000, THE GINGERBREAD HOUSE FEATURED THE SOUTH FRONT of the White House. While I kept the exterior ornamentation minimal, I did place a Christmas wreath on each window and decorated the trees with sprinkles. On the roof a sleigh with nine reindeer waited while Santa Claus read stories to children in the Blue Room. Marzipan figures of Socks and Buddy were positioned near the door.

To observe the last year of the Clinton presidency, the White House Christmas decorations this year recalled all the themes of the past holidays since 1993. For my part, I chose to build a model of the White House exposing three of its rooms—the East Room, Blue Room, and State Dining Room—each decorated to reflect the seven previous Christmas themes of the Clinton administration. On the left, the East Room displayed a traditional Christmas tree and decorations on the mantel as well as a special surprise. In this room I placed miniature replicas of the seven gingerbread houses I made for the Clintons. Re-creating small versions of the past houses was a delight, but took patience! The past Christmas themes were remembered in the Blue Room, while a host of holiday desserts was spread out on the table surrounded by pine trees and poinsettias in the State Dining Room.

Ornaments and decorations from the past seven years of the Clinton administration were placed in each room. The Blue Room (*opposite left*) featured Santa Claus reading "A Visit from Saint Nicholas" and a replica of the 2000 Christmas tree. The State Dining Room (*opposite bottom right*) was filled with poinsettias and pine trees, and set for a buffet of savory desserts. Marzipan Socks and Buddy stood near the foot of the stairs to the South Portico (*opposite top right*). In the East Room (*top*) were miniatures of each house made during the Clinton administration. Before being added to the display, marzipan figures were propped up with styrofoam and toothpicks on trays (*left*).

ANOTHER NEW FIRST FAMILY
HOME FOR THE HOLIDAYS

President George W. Bush was
inaugurated in January 2001. For
the Bushes' first Christmas in the
White House, Chef Mesnier built a
gingerbread house to reflect the
theme of home and family. Here,
First Lady Laura Bush presents
the house to the press.

HOME FOR THE HOLIDAYS

PRESIDENT AND MRS. GEORGE W. BUSH'S FIRST WHITE HOUSE CHRISTMAS was celebrated barely three months after the tragedies of September 11, 2001. The American flag flew prominently on the top of their first gingerbread house.

We again created a view of the South Front, but this time we presented the house as President John Adams would have known it in 1800. The South Portico had not yet been built. There was a staircase from the ground that led to a porch outside the Blue Room, where we placed a group of carolers. On the right side of the lawn, Santa Claus, with his reindeer leading the way, arrived with a sleigh full of presents.

I remember that I decided to add the president's dogs Spot and Barney on the front lawn to personalize the house for the first family. The "Beware of Barney" sign (placed near a marzipan armadillo) was a replica of those placed on the White House lawns to warn squirrels about Barney. He was famous for hunting armadillo in Texas. Beginning in 2002, Barney starred in a series of annual White House holiday videos recorded by the "Barney cam" (right).

Following the national tragedy of September 11, 2001, home and family were on the minds of the American public, and the White House Christmas decorations reflected this. Throughout the house, miniature replicas of eighteen presidents' homes were displayed on the mantels and pier tables. John Adams's Peacefield was placed on the Green Room mantel (*left*). Other replicas included Abraham Lincoln's home in Springfield, Illinois; Lyndon B. Johnson's Texas ranch; Rutherford B. Hayes's Spiegel Grove in Ohio; Andrew Jackson's Hermitage; George Washington's Mount Vernon; and Thomas Jefferson's Monticello.

PRESIDENTIAL PETS

ALL CREATURES
GREAT & SMALL

ALL CREATURES
GREAT & SMALL

IN 2002, WE ONCE AGAIN FEATURED THE SOUTH FRONT of the White House with our gingerbread, but depicted it as it appears today—with the nineteenth-century South Portico and the twentieth-century Truman Balcony included.

Since the White House Christmas theme focused on creatures in the White House, I decided that the South Lawn should be filled with hand-modeled marzipan figures featuring presidential pets. In addition to the cats and dogs we all know and love, some of the other animals included were the Adams alligator, the Madison macaw, the Lincoln turkey, the Hayes Jersey cow and peacock, the Wilson sheep, the Coolidge goose, the Kennedy pony, and the Reagan goldfish.

We also fully decorated the balconies and windows with red and green trees, garlands, and bows. Outside the trees were decorated with golden stars, white doves, and snow-tipped branches.

Marzipan sculptures of past presidential pets positioned in the snow and on the steps of the gingerbread house included many dogs and cats. Of special note were Theodore Roosevelt's pony Algonquin, Rutherford B. Hayes's Jersey cow, and Woodrow Wilson's sheep *(top)*; Calvin Coolidge's white collies, Ronald Reagan's goldfish and the Hayes's peacock *(center)*; John Quincy Adams's alligator, the Kennedys' pony Macaroni, and Old Ike, Wilson's pet ram *(bottom)*.

The marzipan animals made to decorate the 2002 gingerbread house were modeled after animals that past presidents kept at the White House. Clockwise from top left: a flock of White House sheep during the Woodrow Wilson administration, c. 1918; President and Mrs. Calvin Coolidge and their son John with their white collies, Prudence Prim and Rob Roy, 1925; and Algonquin, a calico Icelandic Shetland pony, with Archie Roosevelt in the saddle, 1902.

In 2002 we created a 3-foot-tall chocolate eagle for President George W. Bush. It towered over the buffet table and even the guests. It was so well received that it became a main feature of the holiday pastry table for the rest of the Bush years. This was an incredible task as the eagle was created hand, feather-by-feather, without the use of molds.

The crew in the Pastry Shop assembled for a photograph with the handmade chocolate eagle and buffet they prepared in 2002. From left to right: Jessie Betts, Noree Hathaway, Lindsay Michel, Susie Morrison, Lynn McCartin, Marlene Roudebush, me, Susan Limb, Patrick Musel, Donna Cellere, and Patty Stimmel.

CHRISTMAS WITH CHARACTERS

A Storybook White House

A Storybook White House

FOR MY LAST CHRISTMAS BEFORE I RETIRED from my job as executive pastry chef, I proposed a futuristic gingerbread house to Mrs. Bush. This was something I had always wanted to do. She passed on the idea, however, as she was partial to the traditional gingerbread White House. I agreed and went on to design a gingerbread White House filled with storybook characters that followed along with the White House Christmas theme "A Season of Stories."

For the Storybook Gingerbread House, my assistants and I created marzipan figures of characters from popular children's stories. On the South Side of the White House, the Very Hungry Caterpillar inched along the rooftop railing next to the White Rabbit and the Mad Hatter from *Alice in Wonderland*; Humpty Dumpty sat precariously on the Truman Balcony; and Charlotte weaved her web on the wall. The South Lawn was entirely covered with favorite marzipan characters from books including *Winnie the Pooh*, *The Three Little Pigs*, *The Secret Garden*, *James and the Giant Peach*, *The Cat in the Hat*, *Little Red Riding Hood*, *Jack and the Beanstalk*, and *Rapunzel*. There was even an open window created on the top floor for *Goodnight Moon*—Mrs. Bush's favorite children's book. This gingerbread house was a success and everyone loved looking for his or her favorite storybook characters.

Dozens of characters from everyone's favorite children's books were fashioned in marzipan to fill the grounds, windows, balconies, and even the rooftops of the storybook house. Jack climbed his beanstalk above Gulliver and Little Red Riding Hood (*above*), while the Cat in the Hat performed on the South Lawn (*right*). Peter Rabbit was joined by Cinderella and one of the Three Little Pigs (*opposite*).

I remember that the largest showpiece I ever created for a buffet was a chocolate interpretation of Willy Wonka's Chocolate Factory made at the request of First Lady Laura Bush. We used our imaginations to design the piece, and it was a pastry chef's delight. We used common items such as bowls, bottles, pipes, funnels, and plates to mold the chocolate sections. These molded pieces were then glued together with chocolate. To bring the factory to life, we arranged it to look as if chocolate glaze were being poured onto the cake tops and placed Oompa Loompas on the tops of the machines. Before the centerpiece was moved from the kitchen to the State Dining Room we posted a sign warning staff to be careful when passing by.

The Red & White Gingerbread House

In 2004 Chef Mesnier retired from the White House, but at the special request of First Lady Laura Bush he returned to create one more gingerbread house. Here in 2006 Chef Mesnier puts the finishing touches to the house while cameras are recording.

THE RED & WHITE GINGERBREAD HOUSE

I RETIRED FROM THE WHITE HOUSE in 2004 and was busy with my new career as an author in 2006 when Mrs. Bush asked me to return to make another gingerbread White House. The color scheme was a red and white Christmas. I decided that, keeping with this theme, we would cover the gingerbread White House with individual snowflakes. We made more than 850 of them with royal icing, and just like real ones, each snowflake was unique. They came in all sizes and shapes.

The house was fun to make and looked beautiful. Since it was to be displayed in front of a beautiful antique mirror, I had a great idea. I thought we should glue—with safe royal icing—some snowflakes onto the mirror. It would have created the effect of snowflakes falling through the mirror onto the gingerbread house. But Chief Usher Gary Walters told me it was a very special, old mirror and was not allowed to be touched. I said, "Yes sir. No problem." I did not put any snowflakes on the mirror, but still think it would have looked nice!

2006: THE RED & WHITE GINGERBREAD HOUSE

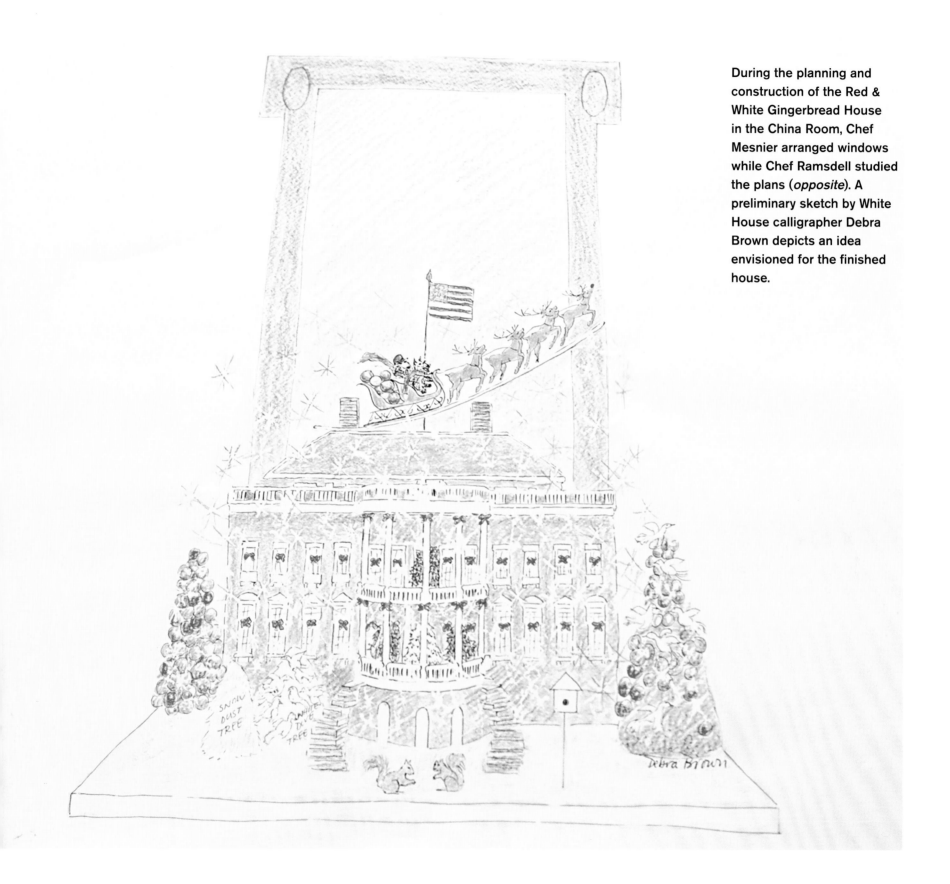

During the planning and construction of the Red & White Gingerbread House in the China Room, Chef Mesnier arranged windows while Chef Ramsdell studied the plans (*opposite*). A preliminary sketch by White House calligrapher Debra Brown depicts an idea envisioned for the finished house.

The White House Operations Crew who moved the heavy gingerbread houses from the Ground Floor to the State Dining Room each year were followed by the press with their cameras, but they were always successful in delivering the house safe and sound for display. In 2006, after the gingerbread house was safely positioned in the State Dining Room, First Lady Laura Bush presented the showpiece to the press.

Making Your Own
Gingerbread House

Plans, Drawings, & Models

Gingerbread Recipes

Shaping & Baking

Decorating Essentials

Preparing to Build

The Showpiece Base

Cutting the Walls

Preparing the Walls, Doors, & Windows

Assembling the House

Special Techniques

Finishing Touches

Plans, Drawings, & Models

BEFORE YOU START BAKING, YOU WILL NEED TO DESIGN YOUR HOUSE and create plans to work from. Good plans will help you immensely and save you time and money. Historical photographs and drawings are good inspiration. The actual blueprints of the building you are going to copy might even be accessible, and you could try to have them output or printed to match the scale of your project. My pastry team and I were fortunate enough to have architectural plans of the White House to reference for our holiday gingerbread houses. When you plan your own gingerbread house, details such as the shape and size of the windows and doors and other significant architectural features should be considered in your early planning. Be sure to capture unique features that define the house. For example, the magnolia tree at the southwest corner of the White House is an identifying feature that I always tried to include in my showpieces.

Good plans will enable you to calculate how much gingerbread you will need to bake. On the following pages we've included edible gingerbread recipes for large and small projects. In addition to drawing plans, it is helpful to make a three-dimensional model of the project you are building. Such a model may be made of foam-core or cardboard and will be helpful in deciding the placement of the gingerbread structure on the base.

Chef Ramsdell and I would consult detailed plans during the construction of the gingerbread houses. In 2006 we referenced architectural drawings of the White House (opposite). Three-dimensional models, like the one pictured below left, were also helpful guides.

Gingerbread for Home Kitchens

The first recipe is suited for the home kitchen and will produce enough gingerbread to make a house using the template provided in the back pocket of this book.

Our White House gingerbread projects required enormous amounts of ingredients. The second recipe is intended for large-scale projects and sized for a 60-quart mixing bowl.

Makes 2 sheets (12 x 18")
Use a 5-quart mixing bowl

¾ cup (1½ sticks) unsalted butter, softened
¾ cup granulated sugar
2 large eggs
5 ounces molasses (liquid measure)
5 ounces honey (liquid measure)
2 teaspoons baking soda
1½ teaspoons cinnamon
1½ teaspoons ginger
⅓ teaspoon salt
6½ cups all-purpose flour

1. Mix all ingredients together in the order listed in the bowl of an electric mixer fitted with the paddle attachment.

2. Let the dough rest and firm up in the refrigerator overnight.

Proceed to instructions for Shaping & Baking on page 118.

Gingerbread for Commercial Kitchens

Makes 12 sheets (18 x 24")
Use a 60-quart mixing bowl

4 pounds unsalted butter, softened
4 pounds granulated sugar
20 large eggs
2 quarts molasses
2 quarts honey
½ cup baking soda
6 tablespoons cinnamon
6 tablespoons ginger
1½ tablespoons salt
20 pounds all-purpose flour

1. Mix all ingredients together in the order listed in the bowl of an electric mixer fitted with the paddle attachment.

2. Let the dough rest and firm up in the refrigerator overnight.

Proceed to instructions for Shaping & Baking on page 118.

Shaping & Baking Gingerbread Sheets

1   Once the gingerbread dough has rested and chilled overnight in the refrigerator, you are ready to shape it for baking. You will be creating a supply of gingerbread "wood" from which to cut out the pieces of the house. When baking in the home kitchen, you should use a flat 12 x 18 inch baking pan—the half size of a professional pan. These pans are readily available at stores and fit most home ovens. It is important that your sheets of gingerbread be smooth, of uniform thickness, and perfectly flat. In order to be successful, you must use flat baking pans. Consider buying a few new baking pans if yours are worn. In the end, you will be glad you did.

2   The gingerbread dough must be rolled flat to a uniform thickness. The gingerbread used for the walls of the house should be ⅜ to ½ inches thick. The gingerbread used for the roof should be ⅜ inch thick. To achieve these precise widths, buy two wooden boards that are the thickness of the walls and the roof. To roll out the dough, begin by placing parchment paper on a flat surface. Dust the paper with flour to prevent the dough from sticking, and then place a brick of dough in center of the parchment paper with your two boards placed at either end of the paper. Put another sheet of parchment paper on top of the dough and, using a rolling pin, roll the dough down to the thickness of the wooden boards. Trim the edges of the dough to fit in the sheet pan. Using the bottom paper, lift the dough and place both the paper and the dough into the sheet pan. Remove the top paper.

3   Dock the dough by pricking holes with a fork all over the top. This will allow steam to escape and help the gingerbread to bake flat. If you do not dock the dough, you will get large bubbles in your gingerbread. Rest the dough in the refrigerator for one hour.

4   Bake at 350 degrees. A half sheet of dough will take about 25 minutes to bake. It is important to bake the dough fully. Bake it to be very dry, as the completed gingerbread house will absorb moisture on humid days. Toward the end of baking, prop the oven door open with a small ball of aluminum foil to allow the steam to escape from the oven. When done, remove the pan from the oven and let the baked dough dry on the sheet pan.

Let your imagination run wild!

The possibilities are endless with gingerbread. It can be baked into a mold of any size or shape that will fit into your oven. One of my favorite examples is seen at left on the Wonderland Castle I made for President and Mrs. Clinton in 1998. I used two French bread molds to make the sides of the tower and glued them together with couverture chocolate.

Details needed to embelish your own house, such as wall textures or roof tiles, can be baked right into your gingerbread sheets. For roof tiles, roll a section of gingerbread dough very thin and then cut out round or square pieces, by hand or with small cookie cutters. Then brush a standard sheet of gingerbread with a light coating of egg wash, and apply your cut tiles on the coated dough in an overlapping pattern. When cooked, the tiles will bake in place as part of the roof (as seen below).

Decorating Essentials

Remember!

· Sift the dry ingredients and strain lemon juice if using icing for fine piping.

· Stir your royal icing frequently as the consistency changes as it rests. Adjust consistency with more sugar or egg whites as needed.

· Royal icing can be piped, spread, or molded.

· Royal icing may be colored. To achieve dark colors, stir in food coloring slowly—do not whip it.

· Royal icing dries very hard.

· A little lemon juice helps the icing to dry faster and makes it harder.

· Keep your bowl of icing covered with a moist towel.

Royal Icing with Egg Whites

4 cups confectioners' sugar, sifted
2 egg whites, strained
Couple of drops of lemon juice

1. Place confectioners' sugar in the bowl of an electric mixer fitted with a paddle attachment.
2. Slowly add egg whites and mix to a smooth consistency.
3. Add lemon juice and mix on medium speed for 10 minutes.

Royal Icing with Meringue Powder

4 cups confectioners' sugar, sifted
5 tablespoons meringue powder
½ cup water

1. Place confectioners' sugar and meringue powder in the bowl of an electric mixer fitted with a paddle attachment.
2. Add water and mix on medium speed for 10 minutes.

Couverture Chocolate

Couverture chocolate contains a high percentage of cocoa solids and cocoa butter, which gives it a richer flavor, and makes it easy to melt and work with. Most important, the cocoa butter crystallizes, allowing the chocolate to harden and remain hard. Although some couverture chocolate can be purchased in stores, it is more practical to order larger quantities through the mail.

ROLLED FONDANT & MARZIPAN

Windows, doors, and other architectural details for your house may be perfectly fashioned from rolled fondant. Decorations such as bows, figures, and greenery may be beautifully made with marzipan. Because of the complexity of making fondant and marzipan at home, we advise you to buy these products ready-made in pastry supply shops or by mail. Check online for sources.

Ready-made marzipan might require preparation before molding. It should be pliable but stiff enough to keep its shape. If it is too dry, add a little heavy syrup 1 teaspoon at a time (*see recipe page 190*). If it is too soft, knead in confectioners' sugar. Take care not to over knead your marzipan or it will release almond oil and it will not be good for modeling; it should feel smooth but not greasy. Food coloring may be kneaded into the marzipan.

Marzipan dries quickly so keep it covered with plastic wrap to keep it moist.

We recommend that you purchase ready-made rolled fondant for use in fashioning such architectural details as the window at left, which is finished with piped royal icing. Ready-made marzipan may be sculpted to create decorations such as our squirrels above.

PREPARING TO BUILD

Warning!

Gingerbread pieces covered with chocolate are delicious and everyone near your workspace will want to eat the scraps. Don't let them! It is important to save all the pieces for such things as the support braces when you start to put the house together.

BEFORE ANY OF THE GINGERBREAD SHEETS WERE MARKED OR CUT, we always strengthened each sheet with tempered couverture chocolate. This critical step was unique to the way I built gingerbread structures at the White House. Gingerbread contains a high percentage of sugar, which is hydroscopic (inclined to absorb moisture). On particularly humid days, a finished gingerbread house may absorb enough moisture to become soft, bend, and even collapse. Humidity is possible in December, especially in Washington, D.C., and the South. We learned that if the gingerbread is supported with a layer of couverture chocolate on its back, the risk of softening and collapse can be almost totally eliminated. When hardened, the chocolate will continue to support the gingerbread walls and structure even if the gingerbread absorbs moisture and becomes soft.

This step is easy. You just have to melt and temper a substantial amount of couverture chocolate. It does not need to be expensive chocolate, but must be couverture and be in temper. Tempering chocolate may seem daunting at first, but once you understand how the process works it will become more fun.

1 The initial melting of chocolate results in fat crystals that separate from the cocoa butter and make the chocolate mix look unattractive. In order to reduce this separation, the chocolate should be melted to a temperature between 100 and 105 degrees for 5 minutes then cooled to 75 to 80 degrees.

2 Slowly increase the temperature to about 88 degrees for semisweet chocolate or 86 degrees for milk and white chocolate. The chocolate should be fluid enough to pipe or spread, but not too hot or it will crystallize. You will need to rewarm the chocolate throughout the process.

3 Whisk briefly for two or three seconds. Make sure the temperature does not rise above 89 degrees. If it does, you will need to start over. It might be best to begin with chocolate that is already in temper (when it does not show gray spots or streaks). When you think the chocolate you are working with is in temper, a good way to test it is to dip a knife into the melted chocolate. If it becomes shiny and hard within a couple of minutes then the chocolate is in temper.

4   When the chocolate is ready, flip a sheet of baked, but cooled, gingerbread onto a flat surface and remove the parchment paper from the bottom. Next ladle enough tempered chocolate to make a layer about ⅛ inch thick. Use an offset spatula to spread the chocolate smoothly over the surface. Cover every inch of the gingerbread so that all of it will be ready to be used when you begin putting together the structure.

5   Watch the chocolate closely. As it starts to harden it will change from a shiny, liquid appearance to an opaque, solid appearance. Flip the gingerbread sheet back over onto a piece of parchment paper with the chocolate side down. As tempered chocolate dries and hardens, it also shrinks. By turning the sheet with the chocolate side down, the gingerbread will stay flat instead of curling up as the chocolate shrinks.

My assistant Marlene Roudebush and I prepared large batches of tempered chocolate to back the gingerbread sheets. This technique made the houses stronger and easier to transport without damage.

THE SHOWPIECE BASE

The Wonderland Castle Gingerbread House shown above illustrates how the abundant use of chocolate, royal icing, and marzipan figures will cover a large base.

EVERY GINGERBREAD HOUSE NEEDS TO BE SET ON A BASE LARGE AND STRONG enough to support it. It must be bigger than the footprint of the house with enough space around it to place decorations. We usually filled the bases around our White House projects with many pounds of chocolate and marzipan decorations. The base must not be bendable and should be made with at least ¾-inch plywood reinforced from below by 2 x 2s or 2 x 4s. If the base bends in any way, the gingerbread house—in spite of its strong construction with tempered chocolate—will probably crack and the decorations of fragile royal icing will likely shatter.

The base should be constructed in a way that allows it to be easily held and moved. When it is time to move the house you will need to find strong helpers, but first make sure you take care to measure doorways, turns in hallways, and other tight spaces on your route to ensure the base will fit through easily. You might even consider putting the base on heavy castors so it can be rolled at least part of the way. Having the base extend farther than the house's footprint, helps solve the problem of movability. At the White House the Operations Crew, numbering at least seven, with help from the Carpenter's Shop and others, moved the gingerbread house year after year. The crew would carry gingerbread houses weighing 200 pounds or more up the North Front steps to a waiting rolling cart by holding the base. They became very accomplished at this task.

It wouldn't have been possible to move our 2001 Home for the Holidays Gingerbread House from the White House China Room to the State Dining Room if it was not secured to a large sturdy base. The bases made for my large-scale projects could reach impressive proportions. The base (below) that held a house I made for a 370-pound gingerbread replica of Mount Vernon in 2009 measured 5 by 9 feet!

CUTTING THE WALLS

ONCE YOUR GINGERBREAD SHEETS HAVE BEEN PREPARED with tempered chocolate, you are ready to cut the major wall sections of the house using your patterns. Experiment with where to place your patterns in order to make the best use of each sheet.

1   Cut the outside walls first. Use the thicker gingerbread sheets for the walls, and save the thinner sheets for the roof. Consider carefully where to cut the sections of a large wall that requires two or more sections. Make the cuts in places where the seams can be hidden by columns or plants. Remember to measure twice and cut once!

2   I suggest investing in a serrated knife or modeler's zip saw. When you cut the gingerbread, make repetitive marks with the knife, sawing until you go the entire way through the gingerbread and the chocolate. Assembly will be easier if you make clean cuts with crisp corners using carpenter squares and metal rulers.

3   Brick outlines can be etched into the surface and highlighted by brushing cornstarch or sugar into the crevices.

I constructed the gingerbread houses in the White House China Room. First I lined up the gingerbread sheets that were coated with couverture chocolate on long tables. I did this with all the sheets we made in order to have them ready and on hand once we started building the walls and roof.

MAKING YOUR OWN GINGERBREAD HOUSE

We used a band saw to cut our gingerbread sheets to size. For smaller projects constructed in the home kitchen, a good serrated knife will work just as well.

We used rotary tools to etch brick outlines, but you can use a small utility knife as well. Stay as true as possible to the building you are trying to model. Keep it simple. The house will be more recognizable if you do so.

Preparing the Walls, Doors, & Windows

THE WINDOWS, DOORS, ARCHITECTURAL FEATURES, and holiday decorations you plan to attach to the outside walls should be prepared next. It is infinitely easier to attach these details while the gingerbread walls are still flat on a table.

1 To prepare the doors and windows, roll out white fondant to be ⅛ inch thick. Make sure to add a light dusting of cornstarch to the surface to avoid sticking.

2 Using a cardboard pattern made from your scale drawings, cut out all windows and doors using a sharp utility knife. The patterns should include casings and architectural molding details. These are things observers will recognize. Let the rolled fondant windows and doors dry for several days on a flat surface before attaching.

3 Before piping the window details, brush the window surface with a light blue powder for added color. Take a small paper cone filled with white, semisoft royal icing (*recipes on page 120*), and pipe the outline of the windows, side casings, and sills directly onto the rolled fondant. Then flood the casing area using a softer royal icing (softness can be adjusted by adding more egg whites). Finally, pipe the window mullions using the first, firmer royal icing. Create similar detailing with royal icing on the doors. Let the windows and doors dry flat for several days.

4   Line up the assembled walls on a flat table—chocolate side down, gingerbread side up. Then place the finished windows and doors where they belong on each section.

5   Refer to your plans often, and measure the windows and doors. Take a step back to look at the arrangement for a clear perspective. When you are sure your placements are perfected, mark the outside of each window and door using a sharp knife.

6   Using a rotary tool or the point of a knife make small, cone-shaped holes beneath where each detail will go. Make two holes for small items and four or more for larger features.

7   Using a small paper bag filled with tempered couverture chocolate, fill each hole until it overflows slightly. Then place a detail on the chocolate and line it up with the knife marks that were made previously. Attach one feature at a time as chocolate, in temper, will set quickly.

8   Watch your tempered chocolate and stir it often. Adjust the temperature up or down as necessary. The entire bowl can easily go out of temper and then you will need to start the whole process over again. After the architectural features are firmly attached, the wreaths, bows, or garlands can be made from royal icing and added.

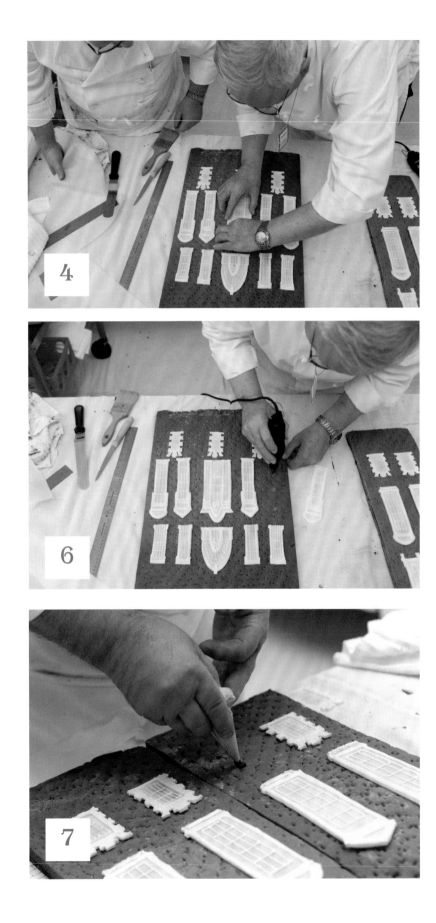

ASSEMBLING THE HOUSE

I T IS NOW TIME TO DECIDE HOW TO POSITION THE HOUSE ON THE BASE. Consider how it will be viewed, whether there are features that jut out, where outside decorations will be placed, and how parts of the house will be reached during its construction. During the construction phase of the project you should have these tools ready: large paper cones; a small fan to accelerate the drying and hardening of the chocolate "glue"; several large carpenters' squares; a rasp; small and large carpenters' levels; and several full boxes of cornstarch and powdered sugar. The squares, levels, and boxes are needed to place the walls at a right angle and brace them while they are being fitted together. Lastly, prepare a large pot of tempered chocolate to have on hand.

Over the years, I needed to use ladders or ask for help from taller assistants when adding the finishing touches to the roofs of the larger gingerbread houses.

RAISING THE ROOF

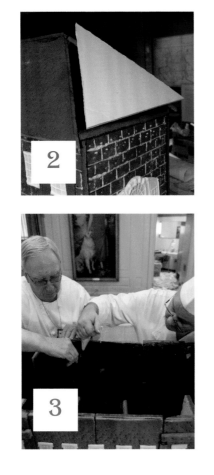

1 First build a gingerbread base for the roof that will enclose the top of the building and sit on the wall braces. Trim the braces with a serrated knife or rasp so the top surfaces are level with the tops of the walls. Make sure the base is level, as the hardened chocolate will prevent you from making any changes.

2 Create patterns for trusses that reflect the shape of the roof using heavy cardboard. Using the patterns, cut the trusses from the gingerbread and glue them to the base of the roof with tempered chocolate. Add bracing to these supports.

3 Cut the roof sections. After trial fitting, glue them in place with generous amounts of chocolate. Make sure the joints have hardened before moving to the next section.

The most difficult part of the gingerbread house construction is building the roof. You need to try to be patient! This step should begin after the walls have been glued together.

3

Special Techniques

5

Replicating the columns of the South Portico required that we develop innovative techniques. The column above was formed in an aluminum foil mold filled with tempered chocolate and rolled in coffee colored marzipan.

THERE ARE TIMES WHEN YOU WILL WANT TO MAKE ROUNDED FEATURES, such as columns, or to smooth a cut edge that does not have the nice appearance of the top of a baked gingerbread sheet. I invented several techniques for these situations that we used in building the White House gingerbread houses. They can be adapted for your projects as well.

Columns

1 To make edible columns, first buy some wooden dowels, with the appropriate diameter for the scale of your project. For White House gingerbread houses, we used ½ to ¾ inch dowels that were slightly longer than the columns would be.

2 Wrap the dowels tightly with several layers of aluminum foil and pinch the foil to close up a bottom end. In the meantime, prepare the tempered chocolate.

3 Carefully pull out the dowel and fill the aluminum foil mold with the tempered chocolate using a paper cone. Hold the tube at an angle so the chocolate flows down one side, allowing the air to escape as the tube is filled up.

4 Stand the filled tubes upright in a bucket and place the bucket in the refrigerator for several hours or overnight to allow the chocolate to fully harden. The foil may then be carefully peeled off to reveal the chocolate column.

5 To make the column look like gingerbread, you can prepare coffee-colored marzipan and roll it into a very thin sheet. Lightly brush the marzipan sheet with water and then roll it carefully around each column. You need to wrap the column with marzipan only once. Measure and fit the columns to the house and glue them in place with the tempered chocolate.

Gingerbread Veneer

6   To make a thin veneer for rounded features or for smoothing cut edges, I use a band saw to cut off a ⅛ inch slice of the finished top surface of a sheet of gingerbread. This veneer sheet is very flexible and can easily be bent around curved forms, such as the Truman Balcony or South Portico. If you do not have a band saw at home, a sharp serrated knife can be used; however, this is a difficult technique and will require patience to master.

7   To make the veneer even more pliable, cover it with a dampened towel until the gingerbread bends easily.

We replicated the porch on the South Front of the White House by cutting several semi-circles of gingerbread and gluing them together, but this left a raw circular front that looked unfinished. The veneer solved this problem.

6

FINISHING TOUCHES

O NCE YOUR HOUSE IS STANDING and the roof, windows, and doors are in place, it is time to add your finishing touches. Have fun! The possiblities are endless. My projects were never finished until I sprinkled powdered sugar over the house to look like fresh fallen snow.

The Red & White Gingerbread House (which I made in 2006 when I returned from retirement) was finished with red bows made of marzipan, hundreds of royal icing snowflakes and icicles, and such surprises as the Bushes' dogs Barney and Miss Beazley taking off in Santa's sleigh, and a tiny dove perched on a birdhouse with India Willie, the Bushes' black cat, lurking below. We even added a red tree of marzipan berries to give color to the snow-covered landscape.

White House Holiday Recipes

Holiday Cookies

Traditional Recipes

Cakes & Soufflés

Meringues, Mousses, & Fillings

Frozen Desserts

Fresh Fruit

HOLIDAY COOKIES

Chef Mesnier, in his White House Pastry Shop, 2001, presents a tray of cookies baked for a reception.

CHRISTMAS COOKIES ARE A SENTIMENTAL PART OF THE HOLIDAYS, and at the White House familiar cookies on the tables make guests from all over the world feel comfortable—almost as if they were at home.

When I was the executive pastry chef, my staff worked to make the guests' buffet experience begin with the smell of fresh-baked cookies. We made many different types of cookies using every production technique available—rolling, cutting, piping, scooping, spritzing, and molding—to create a variety of textures, flavors, shapes, colors, and decorations. They were uniform in size, just enough for one or two bites, so that guests would not have to choose just one large cookie but could enjoy several small cookies instead. The Pastry Shop budget would be stretched to incorporate the very best ingredients—chocolates, dried and glazed fruits, maple sugar, coconut, freshly ground spices, and, of course, a lot of butter and eggs.

Our White House holiday buffets were filled not only with the president's and first family's favorite selections but also with traditional American favorites and many recipes that diplomatic guests would recognize—such as leckerlis and Linzer stars. We took presentation very seriously—preparing each cookie as if it were a gift and one of the many memorable components in what for many guests might be a once-in-a-lifetime experience.

Although we were re-creating the familiar experience of home, there was one very significant difference—the scale! By December 1 of each year I needed 120,000 cookie pieces available in the freezer. From then on, while we drew from our supply of frozen dough, we also continued to prepare more cookie dough every day to bake fresh cookies for each event throughout the holidays. When I came to the White House, cookies were often store bought. I made it my goal to use exclusively fresh-baked cookies for every event. It took six years to achieve this, but with effort and long work hours, we finally did it and continued until I retired. After all, we were baking for the honored guests of the first family.

OAK LEAVES AND MERINGUE ACORNS

Makes 40 cookies

1 cup (2 sticks) unsalted butter, softened
½ cup confectioners' sugar, sifted
4 large egg whites, strained
½ cup all-purpose flour
2 teaspoons cocoa powder

Preheat oven to 350 degrees

1. Cream butter in the bowl of an electric mixer fitted with the paddle attachment.
2. On medium speed, slowly stir in sifted sugar.
3. Continue mixing the batter and slowly stir in the egg whites one tablespoon at a time.
4. Remove the bowl from the mixer. Sift flour onto the mixture and fold into the batter thoroughly.
5. Prepare dark batter to pipe veins in the leaf cookie by removing a few tablespoons of the batter to a separate bowl and stirring in sifted cocoa powder. Set aside.
6. Spread remaining batter onto sheet pans lined with parchment paper and form the shape of an oak leaf using a cardboard or metal stencil.
7. Fill a paper cone with the chocolate batter, cut a small opening, and pipe the veins of the leaf onto the stenciled cookies.
8. Bake cookies until they are lightly brown around the edges, 5 to 8 minutes.
9. Remove the pan from the oven. Let the cookies cool for a few seconds, then carefully remove using a small metal spatula. Twist the warm cookies a little to imitate a curling leaf. Let the cookies cool and harden into different shapes.
10. Put a small dab of tempered chocolate at the base of the cookie leaf and glue on a meringue acorn.

Meringue Acorns

Makes 50 cookies

8 egg whites

1 cup granulated sugar (divided into ½ cups)

1 cup hazelnut flour, lightly toasted

2 cups apricot jam, boiled to reduce
  and thicken, flavored with dark rum

Tempered chocolate (*see page 122*)

Chocolate jimmies

Preheat oven to 300 degrees

1. Place the egg whites in the bowl of an electric mixer fitted with the whip attachment.

2. Whip the egg whites and slowly add in ½ cup sugar. Proceed to form a firm French meringue.

3. Combine the hazelnut flour and the other ½ cup sugar then fold into the French meringue.

4. Place the meringue in a piping bag fitted with a no. 3 or 4 plain round tube.

5. Pipe small ovals onto a sheet pan lined with parchment. They should be approximately 1 x ½ inch.

6. Sprinkle cookies with granulated sugar.

7. Place sheet pan in the oven and bake for 20 minutes, until the cookies are light brown and fully dried.

8. Remove the pan from the oven, and transfer parchment paper with cookies from pan to a wire rack to cool.

9. Take two cookies (the sides of the "acorn") and glue the flat sides together with the reduced apricot jam.

10. Dip the bottom third of the acorn into tempered chocolate and then dip the still wet chocolate in a bowl of chocolate jimmies. Let the chocolate harden.

The preparation of oak leaf and acorn cookies involves making two different recipes, but it is worth the effort! They are an exceptionally beautiful cookies for fall functions and so attractive that your guests may want to keep them as a souvenir.

Coconut Chocolate Squares

Makes 60 squares

PÂTE SUCRÉE, chilled (*double the recipe on page 149*)

FILLING

    4 cups sugar

    12 large egg whites

    5½ cups unsweetened coconut, grated

    ½ teaspoon salt

    1 tablespoon pure vanilla extract

    ¾ cup all-purpose flour

    ½ cup bitter orange marmalade

GANACHE TOPPING

    4 cups semisweet chocolate chips

    2½ cups heavy cream

With the fresh chocolate ganache on top, this cookie is irresistible to everyone who loves coconut and chocolate. Because it freezes well and can be baked in great quantities several months before the holidays, it is ideal for last-minute parties. One Christmas, the President and Mrs. Clinton announced a party for 6,000 guests, with only three days' notice. You better believe these coconut chocolate squares were put to good use!

Preheat oven to 400 degrees

1. Liberally butter a 12 x 18 inch sheet pan.

2. Using plenty of flour on the rolling pin and working surface, roll the pâte sucrée into a rectangle that is 14 x 20 inches. Keep moving the dough around as you roll it so it will not stick to the table.

3. Roll the dough onto the rolling the pin, and then unroll it into the sheet pan. Gently press the dough into the corners of the pan and trim the dough flush with the top, all around the edges. Dock the dough and place the pan in the refrigerator for at least an hour or longer.

4. Line the sheet pan, on top of the dough, with foil or parchment paper. Cover the paper with pie weights or dried beans so the dough will bake flat.

5. Bake for 15 minutes, then carefully remove the weights and paper. Return dough to the oven for about another 15 minutes. Pierce any bubbles that appear in the dough during baking. You want the dough to be light brown all over.

6. Remove pan and baked crust from oven.

Reduce temperature to 300 degrees

7. Begin preparation for the filling. Combine sugar, egg whites, coconut, salt, and vanilla in a metal bowl. Set the bowl on a saucepan that is filled with simmering water. Stir constantly over the heat until the mixture is hot to the touch, between 120 and 130 degrees.

8. Remove the bowl from the heat and stir in flour.

9. Spread orange marmalade evenly over the baked crust.

10. Spread coconut filling evenly over the orange marmalade.

11. Bake for 45 to 60 minutes, until filling is golden brown.

12. Remove pan from the oven and let base cool in the pan completely. At this point the coconut squares can be finished with the ganache topping, or the base can be wrapped and frozen.

13. To finish the squares, prepare the ganache topping. Place the chocolate chips in a large metal bowl. Heat the heavy cream to a simmer and pour over the chocolate. Allow the mixture to set for a few minutes. Then stir until the chips are melted, and the ganache is silky and smooth.

14. Pour the ganache onto the coconut base and spread evenly. Let it cool to room temperature, and then chill overnight before cutting.

15. To serve, remove the pan from the refrigerator. Cut sheet into 60 squares with a large chef's knife that has been dipped in hot water and dried on a towel. Take care to keep the knife hot, clean, and dry. For a cleaner edge, cut the cookies while still cold.

The coconut base—the pâte sucrée with marmalade and coconut—can be baked several months in advance and then frozen. The sheets of coconut base can then be defrosted as needed and finished with a fresh ganache.

FLORENTINE SQUARES

Makes 200 squares

PÂTE SUCRÉE, chilled (*double the recipe on page 149*)

FILLING
    1 cup (2 sticks) unsalted butter
    1 cup granulated sugar
    ½ cup clover honey
    ½ cup heavy cream
    1 tablespoon pure vanilla extract
    Pinch of salt
    2 cups sliced almonds
    ⅓ cup unsalted pistachio nuts
    ⅓ cup dried cranberries, chopped
    ⅓ cup glazed cherries, chopped
    ⅓ cup candied orange peel, chopped
    ⅓ cup dried apricots, chopped

TEMPERED CHOCOLATE, if cookies are footed (*see page 122*)

Preheat oven to 400 degrees

1. Liberally butter a 12 x 18 inch sheet pan.
2. Using plenty of flour on the rolling pin and working surface, roll the pâte sucrée into a rectangle that is 14 x 20 inches. Keep moving the dough around as you roll it so it will not stick to the table.
3. Roll the dough onto the rolling the pin, and then unroll it into the sheet pan. Gently press the dough into the corners of the pan and trim the dough flush with the top, all around the edges. Dock the dough and place the pan in the refrigerator for an hour or longer.
4. Line the sheet pan, on top of the dough, with foil or parchment paper. Cover the paper with pie weights or dried beans so the dough will bake flat.
5. Bake for 15 minutes, then carefully remove the weights and paper and return the dough to the oven for about another 15 minutes. Pierce any bubbles that appear in the dough during baking. You want the dough to be light brown all over.
6. Remove pan from the oven.

Reduce temperature to 375 degrees

7. To prepare the Florentine filling, combine the butter, sugar, clover honey, and heavy cream in a heavy saucepan. Bring the mixture to a boil over medium heat. Stir occasionally and carefully. Cook until the mixture reaches the thread stage, when the syrup drips from a spoon in thin threads, approximately 225 degrees on a candy thermometer, about 6 to 8 minutes.

With a flavor combination and texture unlike any other cookie, Florentine Squares are a delightful addition to any cookie tray.

Though I'm very partial to clover honey, other kinds of honey may be used for variation. Macadamia nuts, hazelnuts, or whole blanched almonds can also be used in the caramel filling.

8. Carefully stir in the vanilla, salt, sliced almonds, pistachios, cranberries, glazed cherries, candied orange peel, and dried apricots. Mix well.

9. Pour the filling over the baked crust and spread evenly with a metal spatula.

10. Bake for another 20 minutes, until surface is bubbling. Bake an additional 2 to 3 minutes until golden.

11. Remove the pan from oven and let it cool completely. The Florentine filling will feel like a soft caramel.

12. To serve, cut the sheet of Florentine into 1 x 1 inch squares.

13. Cut squares may also be "footed" in tempered chocolate. Stick a toothpick into the center of each square. Dip the square in tempered chocolate up to the top edge. Scrape off excess chocolate, on the edge of the chocolate bowl. Deposit dipped squares on parchment paper, remove toothpick handle, and let the chocolate harden.

Pâte Sucrée

1 cup (2 sticks) unsalted butter, room temperature
½ cup granulated sugar
½ tablespoon pure vanilla extract
1 teaspoon grated lemon zest
Pinch of salt
1 large egg
3 cups all-purpose flour

1. Whisk butter and sugar in the bowl of an electric mixer fitted with the paddle attachment and mix until fully combined.

2. Stir in vanilla, lemon zest, and salt until fully combined.

3. Beat egg separately. Add a little bit to the mixture at a time.

4. Add flour, then stir until combined with the mixture.

5. Remove dough from mixer. Dust dough with flour and shape into a smooth ball. Wrap in plastic wrap and chill in the refrigerator overnight.

The cut Florentine squares may be kept in an airtight container for two to three days Uncut squares may be frozen. If they are wrapped well, they will last for up to three months.

These cookies have an unusual melt-in-your-mouth texture. They were always one of the first cookies to be completely devoured at White House holiday parties. Guests rarely ate just one, so we made thousands of them every year and froze them unbaked. Every day during the holidays we baked enough of the frozen hazelnut crescents to serve at the scheduled parties.

Unbaked cookies may be wrapped on a sheet tray and frozen for three months. Defrost the cookies on parchment-lined sheets for 30 minutes at room temperature before baking. Finished crescents will keep for three days in an airtight container at room temperature.

HAZELNUT CRESCENTS

Makes 80 cookies

1 cup (2 sticks) unsalted butter, softened
7 tablespoons granulated sugar
1 large whole egg
1 large egg yolk
1 tablespoon pure vanilla extract
1 tablespoon ground cinnamon
Pinch of salt
2 cups all-purpose flour
1½ cups plus 2 tablespoons hazelnut flour, toasted
1 cup (2 sticks) melted butter for brushing
4 cups confectioners' sugar for dusting

Preheat oven to 375 degrees

1. In the bowl of an electric mixer fitted with the paddle attachment, mix together butter and sugar until well combined and smooth.
2. Slowly stir in the egg and egg yolk. Continue mixing and add vanilla, cinnamon, and salt until well combined.
3. Stir in the all-purpose flour and hazelnut flour until just incorporated.
4. Wrap dough in plasticwrap and refrigerate for at least 2 hours until firm.
5. To shape the cookie, take a heaping tablespoon of dough, or portion the dough with a no. 100 ice cream scoop. Roll the dough between the palms of your hands into a log about 2 inches long, slightly tapered at each end. Gently bend into crescent shapes. Place the crescents on sheet pans lined with parchment paper, spacing them about ¾ inch apart.
6. Bake for 15 minutes, until cookies are light golden brown.
7. Remove pan from the oven and brush the hot cookies lightly with melted butter.
8. Dust heavily with confectioners' sugar using a sieve.
9. Let cookies cool before serving.

RASPBERRY TRUFFLES

Makes 40 truffles

2¼ cups semisweet couverture chocolate, chopped

1½ cups heavy cream

1 cup raspberry jam, sieved

¼ cup raspberry liquor

Tempered chocolate for finishing

Confectioners' sugar for finishing

1. To make the ganache, place chopped semisweet couverture chocolate in dry stainless steel bowl.

2. Place heavy cream in saucepan over medium heat and bring to a boil. Remove from heat immediately when the cream starts to boil around edges.

3. Pour hot cream over the chocolate. Let stand for a couple of minutes and then stir slowly and continually until the chocolate is melted and cream is fully mixed. This is a ganache.

4. Stir in the sieved jam and the raspberry liquor.

5. Let mixture rest until firm enough to hold a shape when piped.

6. Using a pastry bag fitted with a no. 7 round tube, pipe ganache mixture into balls about the size of a large marble. Place on a sheet pan lined with parchment paper.

7. Place sheet pan in the refrigerator for 30 minutes.

8. Spread a layer of confectioners' sugar on parchment paper in a sheet pan.

9. Roll the truffles quickly in the palms of your hands to make them round.

10. Place some tempered chocolate in the palm of your hand. Roll a truffle in the chocolate, adding more chocolate as necessary.

11. Deposit the coated truffle in the confectioners' sugar and roll it around to coat fully.

12. After chocolate has fully set, place a few truffles in a sieve and roll to shake off any excess sugar.

These are delicious little additions to a pastry buffet and always welcomed at the end of a lovely meal.

The finished truffles will keep three to four days at room temperature in an airtight container.

Pecan Diamonds

Makes 120 diamonds

PÂTE SUCRÉE, chilled (*double the recipe on page 149*)

FILLING
  1 cup (2 sticks) unsalted butter
  1¼ cups packed light brown sugar
  ¼ cup granulated sugar
  ½ cup clover honey
  ½ cup heavy cream
  1½ tablespoons pure vanilla extract
  Pinch of salt
  4 cups pecan pieces

1. Liberally grease a 12 x 18 inch sheet pan.
2. Using plenty of flour on the rolling pin and working surface, roll the pâte sucrée into a rectangle that is 14 x 20 inches. Keep moving the dough around as you roll it so it will not stick to the table.
3. Roll the dough onto the rolling the pin, and then unroll it into the sheet pan. Gently press the dough into the corners of the pan and trim the dough flush with the top, all around the edges. Dock the dough and place the pan in the refrigerator for an hour or longer.

Preheat oven to 400 degrees

4. Line the sheet pan, on top of the dough, with foil or parchment paper. Cover the paper with pie weights or dried beans so the dough will bake flat.
5. Bake for 15 minutes, then carefully remove the weights and paper and return the dough to the oven for about another 15 minutes. Pierce any bubbles that appear in the dough during baking. You want the dough to be light brown all over.
6. Remove pan from the oven.

Reduce temperature to 375 degrees

7. To prepare the filling, combine the butter, brown sugar, granulated sugar, clover honey, heavy cream, vanilla extract, and salt in a heavy saucepan Bring the mixture to a boil over medium heat. Stir occasionally and carefully. Cook until the mixture reaches the thread stage, when the syrup drips from a spoon in thin threads, approximately 225 degrees on a candy thermometer, about 6 to 8 minutes.
8   Stir in pecans. Pour the filling over the baked crust and spread evenly with a metal spatula.
9. Bake for another 20 minutes, until surface begins to bubble. Remove the pan from oven and allow cookies to cool thoroughly in the pan.
10. To serve, cut into diamond-shaped pieces approximately 1½ x 1 inch.

Cookies with nuts are very popular, and this cookie is quite easy to make and was very good for serving at large holiday parties at the White House. The diamond shape helps make the cookie trays even more interesting and attractive.

To freeze, wrap the baked cookies on sheets in plastic for up to three months. Defrost in the refrigerator before cutting. Cut pecan diamonds may be kept in a closed container for two to three days.

Linzer Stars and Trees

Makes 40 cookies. Photo page 140.

1 cup (2 sticks) unsalted butter, softened
½ cup granulated sugar
2⅓ cups nut flour—half almond and half hazelnut, lightly toasted
2 large egg yolks
¼ teaspoon salt
2 teaspoons grated lemon zest or 1 teaspoon lemon extract
1½ teaspoons ground cinnamon
1½ cups and 1 tablespoon all-purpose flour

1. Put soft butter, granulated sugar, and nut flours in the bowl of an electric mixer fitted with the paddle attachment. Mix until ingredients are fully combined and smooth.
2. Slowly stir in the egg yolks.
3. Stir in salt, lemon zest, and cinnamon. Mix until fully combined.
4. Add all-purpose flour and stir until just incorporated.
5. Wrap dough in plastic wrap and chill in the refrigerator for several hours.

Preheat oven to 375 degrees

6. Roll out the dough using enough flour to keep it from sticking to your counter. Position two slats of ¼ inch thick wood on either side of your rolling pin to ensure your dough is rolled to ¼ inch thick.
7. Cut out cookies using small star and tree cutters liberally dipped in flour.
8. Place cookies on baking sheets lined with parchment paper.
9. Bake for about 12 minutes, until cookies are golden brown.
10. Remove sheets from the oven and let cookies cool before removing them.
11. Coat cooled cookies with the Christmas cookie glaze, then sprinkle with colored shake-on sugars or nonpareils on top.

These cookies are made from a very flavorful and delicate dough. Baking Linzer cookies makes the whole kitchen smell like Christmas. We frequently made them in the shape of stars and trees, but you can also make other holiday shapes such as reindeer, Santas, snowmen, and wreaths. Tightly wrapped, the cookie dough can be frozen for up to three months. Defrost dough overnight in the refrigerator before shaping. Baked cookies stored in an airtight container will last throughout the holidays.

Christmas Cookie Glaze

2 cups confectioners' sugar
8 egg whites, strained

1. Place egg whites and sugar in a metal bowl and then place over a saucepan of simmering water. Stir by hand until mixture is warm.
2. Place heated mixture into the bowl on an electric mixer fitted with the paddle attachment. Stir on medium speed until glaze is cool, shiny, and smooth.
3. Spread onto cookies.

LECKERLIS

Makes 100 cookies

7¾ cups clover honey
2 cups granulated sugar
11½ cups all-purpose flour
2 cups sliced almonds
5 tablespoons ground cinnamon
2 cups candied orange and lemon peel, chopped
½ tablespoon ground cloves
2½ tablespoons baking soda, mixed with a little milk
¾ cup Kirsch

Preheat oven to 350 degrees

1. Heat honey and sugar in a tall saucepan on medium heat until sugar is dissolved. Make sure you use a tall pot, as honey expands when it is heated.
2. Put hot honey-sugar mixture in the bowl of an electric mixer fitted with the paddle attachment.
3. Mix remaining ingredients and stir into honey sugar until fully combined. You should have dough that is slightly softer than pâte sucrée. Add in a little warm milk, if needed, to achieve the correct texture.
4. Roll out the dough using enough flour to keep it from sticking to your counter. Position two slats of ⅜ inch thick wood on either side of your rolling pin to ensure your dough is rolled to ⅜ inch thick.
5. Roll the dough onto your rolling pin and unroll it onto a 12 x 18 inch sheet pan lined with parchment paper. Thoroughly dock the dough.
6. Bake for 20 minutes. Flip the dough sheet over on to a second cool sheet and return to the oven. Use a small ball of foil to prop open the oven door and allow steam to escape for the entire baking time. Bake for another 10 minutes until golden brown.
7. Remove sheet from the oven and brush any excess flour off the baked dough.
8. Brush the baked dough with the hot leckerli glaze. Flip dough over and brush the glaze on the other side. Move the dough frequently as it cools to keep the glaze from sticking to the baking sheet. Cool completely.
9. To serve, cut cookies in 1½ x 1 inch squares with a serrated knife.

LECKERLI GLAZE

6¼ cups granulated sugar
1 cup water

1. Combine sugar and water in a heavy saucepan.
2. Cook until mixture reaches the thread stage, approximately 225 degrees on a candy thermometer, about 6 to 8 minutes
3. Brush hot glaze onto hot baked dough.

Leckerlis are unique and delicious Swiss cookies. I grew up in France near the Swiss border and I am very partial to them. They have a wonderful crunch, but are still very easy to eat. These delicious cookies, being small and firm, are easy to steal and are favorite targets for cookie thieves—who find their way into every kitchen.

Holiday Buffets and Private Receptions

DURING THE HOLIDAYS, BUFFETS AND PARTIES OCCURRED MORNING, AFTERNOON, AND EVENING, seven days a week. Year after year, as pastry chef for five presidents, I came to know many of the regular guests personally and looked forward to seeing them and watching them enjoy the fruits of our labor.

Group tours were given for special guests, and it was the job of the Pastry Shop to prepare beautiful pastry refreshments and special buffets for them. We knew that the schedule for the very large buffets was set in stone. Notable guests at these events included ambassadors and diplomats, congressmen, members of the press corps, and representatives from all branches of the military. These events were only the tip of the iceberg; additional tours and buffet receptions were added to the schedule as the holidays drew closer.

During November, there were meetings with the first lady and the social secretary to discuss our plans for the buffets and special menu items for particular groups. Though the general framework of buffet menus remained relatively the same from year to year, we always tried to introduce some new items, flavors, presentations, and decorations. We wanted the buffets to be a pleasurable experience for both new and returning guests. I wanted everything to be baked fresh and made with the best ingredients.

The buffets included abundant quantities of traditional desserts such as stollen, buche de Noel, panettone, fruitcakes, and holiday cookies, as well as frozen desserts, warm desserts, bowl desserts, petits fours, chocolate confections, and fresh fruit arrangements. It was important that each dessert could be easily eaten by the guest or taken home as a souvenir of a White House visit.

Throughout each party the buffet tables were kept full, fresh, and clean. The last person to the buffet should have just as wonderful an experience as the first person to the buffet. To ensure this happened, I was present to serve as floor manager. The food and beverage usher Daniel Shanks did a wonderful job overseeing the service staff at the tables. He made sure the Pastry Shop was sufficiently staffed with runners who kept a constant flow of fresh pastries. As trays on the buffet tables became depleted or disheveled, they were removed and replaced with full, perfectly decorated trays. I personally reviewed and approved every item that went to the table.

The White House Pastry Shop was responsible not only for managing large buffets during Christmas but also for serving desserts at private receptions. While buffet desserts were made in small portions and placed on trays, desserts served at private parties were individually plated. They were an opportunity to create dishes that complemented the other courses of the meal. I especially enjoyed the chance to make unique desserts that pleased the first family— whether it was by flavor, color, or decoration. All the skills and talents of the Pastry Shop were used in creating these desserts, and as intended, they brought joy to the guests. We made many desserts over the years and I am pleased to include several of the recipes here to show you the wide range of possibilities in plating a dessert.

Alice from Wonderland, the Mad Hatter, and other papier mâché storybook characters look on as a White House butler arranges a holiday buffet in the State Dining Room prior to the 2003 press preview of the decorations.

Buche de Noel, shaped and decorated to look like a Yule log, was essential for White House holiday buffets. In the example pictured here, the rolled cake is a light sponge roulade moistened with flavored syrup. The icing is a dark buttercream marked to resemble tree bark. The cut ends are coated in vanilla buttercream, and the exteriors are decorated with meringue mushrooms, chocolate, and marzipan details such as holly leaves, berries, stars, wreaths, deer, snowmen, and Santa Claus. The top is dusted with a powdered sugar snow.

BUCHE DE NOEL

5 large eggs, separated
1 tablespoon hot tap water
½ cup sugar
¾ cup all-purpose flour
1 tablespoon finely grated lemon zest
Buttercream, jam, or ganache filling

Preheat oven to 425 degrees

1. Line a half sheet pan or a jelly roll pan with parchment paper and grease paper on pan.
2. Separate the egg yolks and whites into two bowls. Make sure not to let any of the yolk get into the whites.
3. Place the egg yolks in the bowl of an electric mixer fitted with the whisk attachment. Add the hot water and 6 tablespoons of sugar. Whip on high speed until the mixture is pale yellow and creamy, about 7 minutes.
4. Place the egg whites in another bowl of the electric mixer and whip on high speed until they hold soft peaks. Add the rest of the sugar and whip until the egg whites hold firm peaks. Make sure not to overwhip the egg whites or they will be dry.
5. Add the flour and lemon zest to the yolk mixture. Fold lightly with a rubber spatula until they are just combined. Add a scoop of the meringue and fold in. Gently fold the yolk-flour mixture back into the remaining meringue. Do not overfold or it will deflate.

6. Using an offset spatula, spread the mixture on the prepared sheet pan.

7. Bake for 6 to 8 minutes, until the cake is light brown and springs back from the touch.

8. With a small knife, loosen the edges of the cake from the pan. Remove the cake with the parchment paper and let it cool on the paper so it will not dry out.

9. Spread buttercream, jam, or ganache filling on the middle portion of the cake and roll up until the two ends meet.

10. Let the cake firm up in the refrigerator for at least an hour before serving.

ENGLISH COFFEE BUTTERCREAM

3 cups (6 sticks) unsalted butter, softened
2 cups whole milk
¾ finely ground coffee beans (see alternatives in note at right)
8 large egg yolks
2 cups sugar

1. Combine the whole milk and ground coffee in a saucepan. Bring to a boil, then remove the pan from heat and steep for 10 minutes. Pour mixture through a very fine sieve. Make sure you have two cups of liquid. Add more milk if needed.

2. Return the milk to the saucepan and bring to a boil again. Remove from heat.

3. Whisk the eggs yolks and sugar in the bowl of an electric mixer fitted with the whisk attachment. While whisking, dribble in half of the hot milk and coffee in small amounts at a time. Make sure the sugar has dissolved.

4. Pour the egg mixture back into the remaining milk in the saucepan. Reduce heat to low. Stir constantly with a wooden spoon or spatula until little bubbles start to form around the edge from the heat, but do not let the mixture come to a complete boil. Strain mixture into a bowl and cool to room temperature.

5. Place butter in the bowl of an electric mixture fitted with the whisk attachment, and whip on high speed until it is light and fluffy. Slowly add the cold custard and whip until blended. When finished the buttercream will be light and smooth.

I often filled the traditional buche de Noel dessert with buttercream custard fillings. This recipe for a coffee buttercream was a favorite with the White House guests. Other flavors you can use are rum, chocolate, or hazelnut. If you do not like buttercream, then ganaches or jams are also wonderful in this dessert. The English coffee buttercream can be refrigerated for three days. When ready to use, bring to room temperature and whip again.

Eggnog

Eggnog is a holiday treat that adds a special touch to the evening by encouraging toasts and storytelling. This recipe is rich and creamy and contains the traditional spirits. The added whipped cream and meringue lighten the taste and makes the eggnog thicken nicely as it chills. It becomes so thick it is almost like eating ice cream. Many White House guests who didn't think they liked eggnog enjoyed this recipe immensely.

Serves 12

1 quart cold heavy cream
10 pasteurized egg yolks (it is important to use pasteurized, not raw, eggs)
10 large egg whites
2 tablespoons superfine sugar
⅓ cup granulated sugar
1½ cups blended whiskey
¾ cup dark Jamaican rum
2 cups cold milk
¾ cup heavy syrup (*see page 190*)
Grated rind of 1 orange
Grated rind of 1 lemon
Ground nutmeg

1. Place the cold heavy cream in a 2 gallon punch bowl. Fold together the whipped yolks, whipped heavy cream, and whipped egg whites, and beat by hand until the cream doubles in volume and holds soft peaks.
2. In a separate bowl, whip the yolks on high speed until they are light and very thick.
3. Place the egg whites in the bowl of an electric mixer fitted with the whisk attachment. With the mixer on high, add the ⅓ cup granulated sugar and whip the egg whites until they hold very soft peaks.
4. Pour the foamy egg whites into the whipped yolks and mix until they are thoroughly combined.
5. Slowly stir in the heavy syrup, whiskey, dark rum, and cold milk.
6. Sprinkle the top of the eggnog with the orange zest, lemon zest, and grated nutmeg.
7. Place the punch bowl in the refrigerator and chill for at least 4 hours or overnight. The eggnog will thicken as it chills.

PANETTONE

I often included two traditional holiday breads, panettone and stollen, on the buffet trays. I would always serve panettone cut in bite-sized slices. It can also be served toasted with butter and sugar on top.

DOUGH

- 4 cups all-purpose flour
- ½ cup granulated sugar
- 2 teaspoons salt
- 5 large egg yolks, room temperature
- 1 large whole egg, room temperature
- 2 cubes fresh yeast or 3 teaspoons dried yeast, dissolved with 3 tablespoons lukewarm water
- ¾ cup plus 1 tablespoon milk
- ¼ cup vegetable oil
- 1 cup (2 sticks) unsalted butter, softened

FRUIT FILLING

- ½ cup candied orange and lemon peel, chopped
- ½ cup golden raisins, soaked in fresh cider for several months, drained
- ½ cup pistachios, chopped
- Dash of pure vanilla extract
- 1 teaspoon almond extract (or less; use at your discretion)
- 1 teaspoon lemon oil
- Zest of 1 orange and 1 lemon

1. Place the flour, sugar, and salt in the bowl of an electric mixer fitted with the paddle attachment. Using medium speed, slowly add egg yolks and whole egg for a firm elastic dough, mixing for 5 to 7 minutes.
2. Stir the yeast into the dough.
3. Combine the milk and vegetable oil. Slowly add this mixture to the dough. Knead for 10 minutes with the mixer using the dough hook attachment.
4. On medium speed, add the butter one tablespoon at a time.
5. Place the dough in a bowl and seal with plastic wrap. Let the dough rise until it doubles.
6. Fully deflate the dough by punching it several times.
7. Prepare the fruit filling by mixing the ingredients together and then mix the fruit filling into the finished dough.

Preheat oven to 400 degrees

8. Grease a tall cylindrical mold and fill halfway with the dough. Let the dough double and brush the top with the egg wash. Dip scissors in water and cut an X into the top of the dough to release steam. Bake for 15 minutes.

Reduce temperature to 350 degrees

9. Bake dough for another 40 minutes.
10. Remove mold from the oven and brush the top of the panettone with melted butter. After cooling, remove the panettone from the mold and serve.

STOLLEN

DOUGH

1½ cups all-purpose flour
½ cup bread flour
¼ cup granulated sugar
1½ teaspoons salt
¼ cup almond paste
I teaspoon grated nutmeg
1 cup milk
1 whole egg
1 egg yolk
¼ cup fresh yeast
½ cup clarified butter

MIXTURE 1
Combine the following ingredients:

1 tablespoon almond paste, diluted with milk
1 tablespoon granulated sugar
½ teaspoon salt
1 teaspoon stollen spices

MIXTURE 2
Combine the following ingredients:

1 cup all-purpose flour
¼ cup milk
¼ cup clarified butter
½ cup raisins
1½ tablespoons candied lemon peel, chopped
1½ tablespoons candied orange peel, chopped
½ tablespoon lemon oil
¼ cup sliced almonds

FINISHING TOUCHES

½ pound clarified butter, melted
1 pound confectioners' sugar

Our stollen recipe requires the use of fresh yeast, which yields a better taste than dry yeast. It is also called compressed yeast. It is available in cakes and must be refrigerated.

1. First prepare the dough. Place the all-purpose flour, bread flour, sugar, salt, almond paste, and nutmeg in the bowl of an electric mixer fitted with the paddle or dough hook attachment. On medium speed, mix until the ingredients are fully combined. Slowly add the milk to make a firm dough. Add the eggs and continue to kneed for 5 minutes with mixer. Stir in the yeast and soften with some water. Knead the dough for 10 minutes. Stir in the clarified butter. The dough is ready when the butter is fully incorporated.
2. Add MIXTURE 1 to the dough and put in a bowl, cover with plastic wrap, and set aside until the dough doubles in size.
3. Deflate the dough and stir in MIXTURE 2.
4. Cut the dough into two pieces. Shape each piece into long ovals about 12 inches long and 5 inches wide. Flatten the dough slightly with a rolling pin and press a trench into the dough just off center. Take the smaller half and fold it over the trench and press lightly into the bottom half.
5. Place the stollen on a sheet pan lined with parchment paper, cover lightly with plastic wrap, and let it fully rise, until it doubles in size.

Preheat oven to 375 degrees

6. Bake for 1 hour or until a toothpick inserted in the center of the stollen comes out clean.
7. Remove pan from the oven and immediately brush the stollen with melted, clarified butter.
8. Sieve powdered sugar over the butter, covering the bread completely.

STOLLEN SPICES

1 cup cinnamon
¼ cup nutmeg
¼ cup ginger
¼ cup cloves
¼ cup allspice
¼ cup mace
½ tablespoon cardamom

Mix spices together and store in a closed container.

Fruit Cake

Serves 20

3 tablespoons dry sherry
3 tablespoons brandy
2 tablespoons diced dried pears
⅓ cup diced glazed fruit
⅓ cup dark raisins
⅓ cup dried currants
3 tablespoons dried cranberries
3 tablespoons dried cherries
2 tablespoons dried blueberries
1½ tablespoons candied lemon peel, chopped
1½ tablespoons candied orange peel, chopped
8 tablespoons (1 stick) unsalted butter, softened
¼ cup granulated sugar
¼ cup packed light brown sugar

3½ tablespoons all-purpose flour
½ tablespoon pure vanilla extract
1 teaspoon almond extract
1 teaspoon ground cinnamon
1 teaspoon ground nutmeg
Pinch of salt
1 tablespoon plus 1 teaspoon honey
2 large eggs
¾ cup cake flour
1 teaspoon baking powder
1 teaspoon lemon extract
⅓ cup pecans, coarsely chopped
⅓ cup dark rum
¼ cup apricot jam
½ rum glaze recipe

After tasting this, you will no longer hate fruitcake—I promise! We often included slices of fruitcake on buffet cookie trays as pictured opposite, third dessert from the left. This tray also includes slices of stollen, sixth dessert from left.

Rum Glaze

Mix together:

1 cup confectioners' sugar
1 tablespoon dark rum
1 tablespoon water

1. Combine sherry, brandy, pears, glazed fruit, dark raisins, currants, cranberries, cherries, blueberries, and lemon and orange peel in a large bowl. Stir with wooden spoon to combine, wrap with plastic, and let stand overnight.

Preheat oven to 400 degrees

2. Grease a 10 x 4 inch pan and line with parchment paper.
3. Place butter, granulated sugar, and brown sugar in the bowl of an electric mixer fitted with the paddle attachment. Mix on medium speed until ingredients are nicely blended together.
4. With machine on slow speed, stir in the all-purpose flour until combined. Add vanilla extract, almond extract, cinnamon, nutmeg, and salt. Stir in honey and eggs one by one until blended.
5. Sift baking powder into cake flour and add to above mixture, along with pecans, and lemon extract. Mix until fully incorporated.
6. Remove bowl from mixer and stir in the chilled fruit mixture by hand.
7. Pour cake mixture into the prepared loaf pan. Reduce temperature to 350 degrees and bake for 1 hour, or until a toothpick inserted in the center of the cake comes out clean.
8. Remove pan from the oven and leave the cake in the pan. Drizzle dark rum over cake while still hot.
9. Bring the apricot jam to a boil in a saucepan, strain into a bowl, and pour over cake. Brush with the rum glaze last. Let the cake cool before removing it from the pan.
10. For best results, wrap well in plastic wrap and refrigerate for at least two weeks, or up to a year.

This star-shaped cake delighted guests with three delicious layers of flavors: spice cake topped with passion fruit mousse (page 186) and mascarpone mousse (page 184).

SPICE CAKE

¼ cup raisins, chopped

2 tablespoons plus 1 teaspoon candied orange peel, finely chopped

½ teaspoon grated lemon zest

½ teaspoon grated orange zest

6 tablespoons plus ¾ cup cake flour

1 teaspoon baking powder

½ teaspoon baking soda

1 teaspoon ground cinnamon

1 teaspoon ground ginger

½ teaspoon ground cloves

½ teaspoon ground allspice

Pinch of ground nutmeg

8 tablespoons unsalted butter, softened

5 tablespoons granulated sugar

5 tablespoons light brown sugar

2 large eggs, room temperature

1 large egg yolk, room temperature

5 tablespoons buttermilk, room temperature

Preheat oven to 375 degrees

1. To prepare the bottom layer spice cake, use a 10 inch star-shaped pan. Line bottom with greased parchment paper.

2. Stir raisins, candied orange peel, lemon and orange zest, and 1 teaspoon cake flour together in a bowl and set aside.

3. Sift the remaining cake flour (¾ cup plus 1 tablespoon and 2 teaspoons) with baking powder, baking soda, cinnamon, ginger, cloves, allspice, and nutmeg in a separate bowl.

4. In the bowl of an electric mixer fitted with the paddle attachment, blend 5 tablespoons of the butter, the granulated sugar, and light brown sugar. Stir on medium speed until smooth. Stir in the eggs, one at a time, and then the yolk.

5. Slowly stir one-quarter of the flour mixture made in step 3 and add 2 tablespoons of the buttermilk. Continue this process, alternating the addition of wet and dry ingredients. Make sure to end with the flour. Stir in the raisin mixture.

6. Pour the mixture into the star-shaped pan and bake for 30 to 40 minutes, until a toothpick inserted in the middle of the cake comes out clean.

7. Remove pan from the oven. Run knife around edge of cake to loosen it. Invert cake onto cooling rack, lift off pan, and leave cake to cool.

8. To make a passion fruit mouse cake, spread an inch thick layer of passion fruit mousse (*recipe on page 186*) on top of spice cake so it becomes the middle layer. Add the mascarpone mousse (*recipe on page 184*) an inch thick on top of the passion fruit mousse to form the final layer.

9. Serve with fresh fruit on the side.

Chocolate Soufflé Roulade

SOUFFLÉ
- 1 cup semisweet chocolate, finely chopped
- 8 large egg whites
- ¾ cup granulated sugar
- 6 tablespoons all-purpose flour
- ¼ cup seedless raspberry jam
- 2 cups heavy cream
- 3 tablespoons confectioners' sugar

GANACHE GLAZE
- 1½ cups semisweet chocolate chips
- 1 cup and 6 tablespoons heavy cream

GARNISH
- 1 pint raspberries

Preheat oven to 425 degrees

1. Grease a half sheet pan or a 12 x 16 inch jelly roll pan and line with parchment paper.
2. Put 2 inches of water in a saucepan and bring to a simmer. Place the chocolate in a bowl over simmering water. Stir until chocolate is melted and smooth. Remove from heat and cool.
3. Place the egg whites in a separate bowl of an electric mixer fitted with the whisk attachment, and whip on high speed until soft peaks form. On high speed, mix in the sugar and continue to whip until the meringue holds firm peaks.
4. On low speed, add in flour, then mix on high for 10 seconds.
5. Remove the bowl from the mixer and fold in the melted chocolate.
6. Using a piping bag fitted with a plain round ⅝ inch tip, pipe the meringue batter into the pan. Pipe long straight lines horizontally until the whole pan is filled. Bake for 12 to 15 minutes, until the meringue is firm to the touch. Do not push too hard as the meringue will still be slightly soft in the middle. Remove pan from the oven and let the meringue cool in the pan.
7. Invert the cooled cake onto parchment paper sprinkled with granulated sugar. Carefully remove the parchment paper from the meringue cake. Spread on the raspberry jam.
8. Whip the heavy cream and the confectioners' sugar in the bowl of an electric mixer fitted with the whisk attachment. Spread whipped cream over the jam and distribute the raspberries on top.
9. Starting along the long edge, and using the parchment as a guide, roll up the cake. When rolled up, center it on the parchment and fold the parchment over the cake towards you. Hold the bottom parchment and put a ruler on the top. Push toward the bottom edge of the cake to tighten. Then roll the cake in the parchment and twist the end to tighten the roll. Let the cake chill and firm up in the refrigerator for at least an hour.
10. To finish the cake, prepare the ganache topping. Place the chocolate chips in a large metal bowl. Heat the heavy cream to a simmer and pour over the chocolate. Allow the mixture to set for a few minutes. Then stir until the chips are melted, and the ganache glaze is silky and smooth. Place the souffle on a wire rack set on a sheet pan and brush several times with the glaze and garnish with fresh raspberries.
12. Decorate the cake for the holidays with chocolate and marzipan decorations.

The chocolate soufflé roulade used to make the buche de Noels (above) for a friends and family event during the George H. W. Bush administration was quite large—18 inches long—and served about 60 people. Marzipan decorations were arranged on top of the Yule log dessert to create a miniature woodland scene. The sides were garnished with fruit or toasted pumpkin seeds.

Orange Sabayon Cake

DOUGH
    1¾ cups plus 2 tablespoons cake flour
    1 teaspoon baking soda
    Pinch of salt
    7½ tablespoons unsalted butter, softened
    11 tablespoons sugar
    2 tablespoons frozen orange juice concentrate
    1½ teaspoons grated orange zest
    1 large whole egg
    2 large egg yolks
    ⅓ cup milk

SAUCE
    1½ cups light syrup (4 cups water and 2 cups granulated sugar), warmed
    ⅓ cup Grand Marnier

GANACHE
    3 cups semisweet chocolate chips
    2 cups heavy cream

MOUSSE
    1 cup heavy cream

Preheat oven to 375 degrees

1. Grease and flour a 9-cup bundt pan.
2. Sift 1 cup plus 2 tablespoons of cake flour, baking soda, and salt, then set aside.
3. In the bowl of an electric mixer fitted with the paddle attachment, combine the butter, 6 tablespoons of sugar, ¾ cup of cake flour, orange juice concentrate, and orange zest. Beat until smooth and creamy.
4. In a separate mixer bowl, combine the egg, egg yolks, and 5 tablespoons of sugar. Beat on high speed until a pale color, about 7 minutes.
5. Fold the egg mixture into the butter mixture. Mix in one-third of the milk and one-third of the flour mixture. Continue this process, making sure the flour is the last ingredient added.
6. Pour mixture into the bundt pan and bake for 20 minutes, until a toothpick inserted in the center of the cake comes out clean.
7. Remove from the oven and allow the cake to cool in the pan.

8. To finish the cake, combine the light syrup and Grand Marnier and dribble over the cake while it is still in the mold, until all syrup is absorbed. Invert the cake and place on a serving platter.

9. Heat one cup of the heavy cream and pour over chocolate chips. Blend until smooth to form a ganache and brush one cup all over the cake.

10. Whip the rest of the heavy cream until firm peaks form and fold into the remaining (cooled) ganache topping to make a mousse. Using a piping bag fitted with a large star tip, fill the center of the cake and then pipe a shell border around the cake.

11. Decorate the cake as appropriate for the holidays.

Cherry Trifle with Port Wine

This holiday dessert can be made well in advance of serving and tastes even better after being refrigerated for 3 to 4 days to give the flavors time to develop. The final génoise cake may be wrapped and frozen up to a month.

GÉNOISE
4 large eggs
½ cup granulated sugar
¾ cup plus 1½ tablespoons all-purpose flour
Pinch of salt
1 teaspoon pure vanilla extract
4 tablespoons unsalted butter, melted *(optional)*

PASTRY CREAM
¾ cup plus 2 tablespoons granulated sugar
½ cup plus 2 tablespoons cornstarch
5 large whole eggs, or 8 large egg yolks
1 quart milk
1 tablespoon pure vanilla extract
Pinch of salt
4 tablespoons unsalted butter, chilled *(optional)*

TRIFLE
One 8 or 9 inch round génoise
½ cup seedless raspberry jam
½ cup Port wine
1 cup heavy cream, chilled
2 cups pastry cream
Two 14-ounce cans sweet black cherries, pitted, drained, and patted dry

Preheat oven to 375 degrees

1. First make the génoise. Grease a 9 x 2 inch round pan, line bottom of pan with parchment, and grease paper. Dust inside paper with flour.

2. Place two inches of water in a saucepan and bring to a simmer. Put the eggs and sugar in the bowl of an electric mixer and place over the simmering water. Whisk by hand until it is fully combined and warm.

3. Place the bowl back on the electric mixer fitted with the whisk attachment and whip on high speed for 5 minutes. The mixture will increase in volume and become cool.

4. Reduce the speed to low and mix for another 12 minutes. The mixture will now become thick and shiny.

5. Using a rubber spatula, fold in the flour and mix, then fold in the vanilla and salt. Add butter, if desired.

6. Pour the mixture into the prepared cake pan. Bake for 22 to 25 minutes. When finished, the cake should be firm to the touch and a toothpick inserted in the center of the cake should come out clean. Remove pan from the oven.

7. Let the cake cool fully. Invert the cake when removing from pan.

8. Now it is time to make the pastry cream. In a medium bowl, whisk together the granulated sugar and cornstarch by hand. Add the eggs or yolks and whisk.

9. Heat the milk in a non-aluminum saucepan until it reaches a boil. Remove from the heat and slowly add it to the egg mixture, one half cup at a time, whisking constantly by hand. After adding half of the milk to the eggs, whisk to make sure everything is combined.

10. Pour the egg mixture back into the saucepan with the remainder of the milk and whisk to combine. Return pan to the heat and slowly bring to a full boil, whisking constantly.

11. Pour into a bowl and stir in vanilla, salt, and butter until cool.

12. Before using, push chilled pastry cream through a sieve and stir until smooth.

13. To finish, using a serrated knife, cut the génoise layer into three layers of equal thickness, each about ¾ inch. Spread a quarter of the raspberry jam on the tops of two layers. Restack as a jam layer cake and cut the assembled cake into 1 inch cubes.

14. Now it is time to prepare the trifle. Place the cubes in a bowl and sprinkle with ¼ cup of the Port. Stir gently to make sure the cubes are moist.

15. Whip the pastry cream in the bowl of an electric mixer fitted with the whisk attachment until it holds a soft peak. In a separate bowl, whip the heavy cream until it forms soft peaks. Stir another ¼ cup of Port into the pastry cream and then fold into the whipped cream.

16. Arrange the cubes of cake on the bottom of a serving bowl. Cover cubes with a layer of the pastry cream and add cherries on top. Repeat this process until everything has been used. Make sure to end with a layer of cream and garnish with 12 or more cherries.

Honey Custard Ring with Meringue Christmas Tree

½ cup granulated sugar

½ cup water

6 large whole eggs

2 large egg yolks

1 cup honey

1 quart 2 percent milk

2 vanilla beans, split lengthwise

3 cups of fruit, cut into bite-size pieces

Meringue Christmas Tree (*page 174*)

Preheat oven to 375 degrees

1. Combine sugar and ¼ cup water in a saucepan. Bring mixture to a boil and cook, without stirring to very dark amber. Remove from heat and very carefully pour in ¼ cup water. Stir mixture with a long spoon. Be careful as the hot sugar will foam up and splatter. When caramel is smooth and no longer bubbling, pour into an 8 inch savarin mold. Set aside to cool completely.

2. In a bowl, whisk together eggs, yolks, and honey.

3. Place milk in a saucepan. With a paring knife, split open the vanilla beans length-wise and scrape out the seeds. Add seeds and cut beans to the milk. Heat milk slowly to a boil. Immediately remove pan from heat and let the mixture steep for 5 minutes.

4. Slowly whisk the milk into the egg mixture to make a custard and then strain through a fine sieve. Pour the custard into a savarin mold.

5. Place the savarin mold into a roasting pan with high sides lined with two layers of brown paper. Add enough hot tap water to come three-quarters of the way up the sides of the mold.

6. Place roasting pan in the oven and cover with a sheet pan. Bake the custard ring for 25 to 35 minutes until the custard is set at the edges but still soft in the middle.

7. Remove roasting pan from the oven and let the custard cool, in the water bath, for 45 minutes. Remove savarin mold from pan and cool completely.

8. To serve, place a service plate on the savarin mold, invert, and lift off the mold.

This dessert was Mrs. Carter's favorite, so I made it for her every Christmas she was at the White House. Once baked, the honey custard ring can also be served with fruit salad on the side.

Meringue Christmas Tree

The simplicity of this dessert makes it very special. The distinctive textures of the two very straightforward recipes, custard and meringue make it silky and crunchy at the same time. Needless to say it was a popular dessert on the buffet. Our wonderful White House butlers would be available to help guests who were afraid to damage the beautiful tree, which was served from the top down.

8 large egg whites
2 cups granulated sugar
1 cup whipped cream
cocoa powder for dusting

Preheat oven to 200 degrees

1. Combine the egg whites and sugar in the bowl of an electric mixer fitted with the whisk attachment. Place the mixing bowl on a saucepan of boiling water. Be careful that the hot water does not touch the bottom of the bowl. Stir the egg whites and sugar mixture until it becomes very warm, about 125 to 130 degrees.

2. Return the bowl to the mixer and whip on high speed until the meringue is cool, with firm peaks, and shiny.

3. Using a piping bag fitted with a large no. 7, plain round tube, pipe the layers of the Christmas tree onto parchment-lined sheet pans in a ringed pattern.

4. Place the sheet pans in the oven and prop the oven door open with a small ball of aluminum foil to allow moisture to escape. Keep meringues in oven for 2 to 3 hours, until completely dry. Remove from the oven and cool on trays.

5. Stack the dried layers of meringue to form a Christmas tree, gluing each layer together with whipped cream. Place the meringue tree on top of the custard ring. Dust with cocoa powder.

LIGHT LEMON BOURBON SAUCE

This sauce works best when paired with a warm dessert such as a cobbler, soufflé, or bread pudding.

1 tablespoon cornstarch

½ cup sugar

1 cup boiling water

3 tablespoons fresh lemon juice

1 teaspoon grated lemon zest

2 tablespoons unsalted butter

¼ cup bourbon

1. Mix the cornstarch and sugar in a small saucepan.
2. Whisk in the boiling water. Bring mixture to a boil for several minutes until the sauce thickens.
3. Remove from heat and stir in the lemon juice, lemon zest, and butter.
4. Stir in the bourbon and whisk until combined.

We called our 10 gallon mixing bowl at the White House the "super bowl." It was large enough to make 18 2-quart gingerbread soufflés. For a large State Dinner I would need to produce 26 soufflés and so I would make two batches in this bowl. I used my hands to reach to the bottom of the bowl to be sure it was thoroughly mixed.

Gingerbread Soufflé

¼ cup unsalted butter, softened

½ cup all-purpose flour

3 tablespoons light brown sugar

½ tablespoon ground ginger

½ teaspoon ground cinnamon

½ teaspoon ground nutmeg

2 tablespoons crystallized ginger, finely chopped

Pinch of salt

1 cup milk

5 large egg whites

4 large egg yolks

¼ cup of sugar

Preheat oven to 400 degrees

1. Butter 12 half-cup soufflé molds and sprinkle with sugar.
2. Mix the soft butter with the flour, brown sugar, ginger, cinnamon, nutmeg, crystallized ginger, and salt to form a beurre manié.
3. Place the milk in a saucepan and bring to a boil. Whisk in the beurre manié and stir until it forms a creamy sauce.
4. Transfer the sauce to a large bowl and stir in one egg white. Whisk in the yolks one at a time.
5. In a separate bowl, whip the rest of the egg whites, while adding the sugar, to create firm peaks.
6. Fold the meringue into the yolk mixture.
7. Fill the prepared soufflé molds to the tops. Place the soufflé molds in a hot water bath and bake for about 12 minutes.
8. Remove molds from the oven and let rest for 5 minutes.
9. Serve in or out of the molds with the light lemon bourbon sauce (*see recipe page 176*).

This soufflé uses a traditional white sauce base, heavily seasoned with gingerbread spices. It has the consistency of a very moist, light pudding, and can be served from the mold or inverted and used for individual plating. The lemon bourbon sauce served on the side highlights the seasonal flavors of the soufflé.

This is one of the lightest desserts I served at the White House and a favorite of Nancy Reagan and her special guests.

Raspberry Sauce

1½ pounds fresh raspberries or two 12 ounce bags of frozen, unsweetened raspberries, thawed

½ cup granulated sugar

Combine the raspberries and sugar in a blender and blend until smooth. Push the mixture through a fine-mesh strainer into a bowl. Use immediately, refrigerate in an air-tight container for up to 2 days, or freeze for up to 3 weeks.

Meringue Roses

8 large egg whites, at room temperature
1 cup plus 1½ tablespoons granulated sugar
Raspberry Sauce (optional)

1. Place the egg whites in the bowl of an electric mixer fitted with the whisk attachment, and whip on high speed until soft peaks form. With the mixer running on high, slowly and steadily run the sugar into the whites. Continue whipping until a meringue forms. It will be shiny and hold firm peaks.

2. Put the meringue in a pastry bag fitted with a large no. 104 petal tip.

3. Cut small squares of parchment paper—about 3 x 3 inches—and grease the papers with vegetable shortening.

4. Place 3 inches of water in a large sauce pan and bring to a simmer.

5. Pipe a rose onto each paper petal by petal.

6. Place each piece of parchment paper on the simmering water and let the rose slide off. Cover the poaching pan. This will allow the roses to be poached on the bottom and steamed on the top, thereby avoiding the need to turn them over. Let the meringue roses float in the covered pan for 45 seconds to 1 minute.

7. Carefully lift the poached roses from the water with a slotted spoon and place on dry kitchen towel.

8. Serve immediately with raspberry sauce if desired or store uncovered in refrigerator for two to three hours.

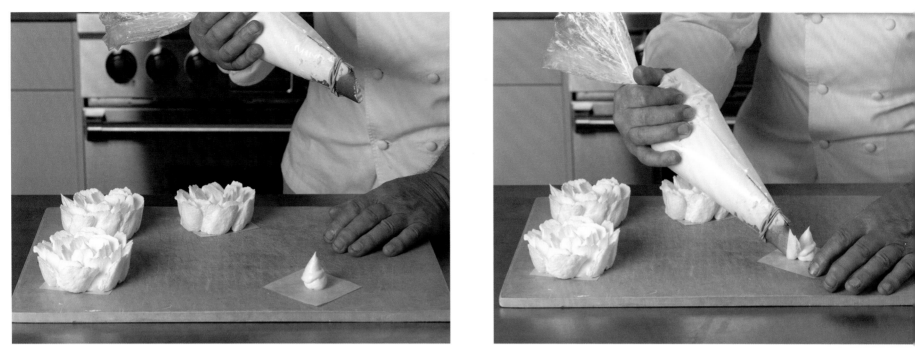

Pipe the roses onto squares of parchment paper petal by petal.

Remove the poached roses from the water with a slotted spoon and place on dry kitchen towel.

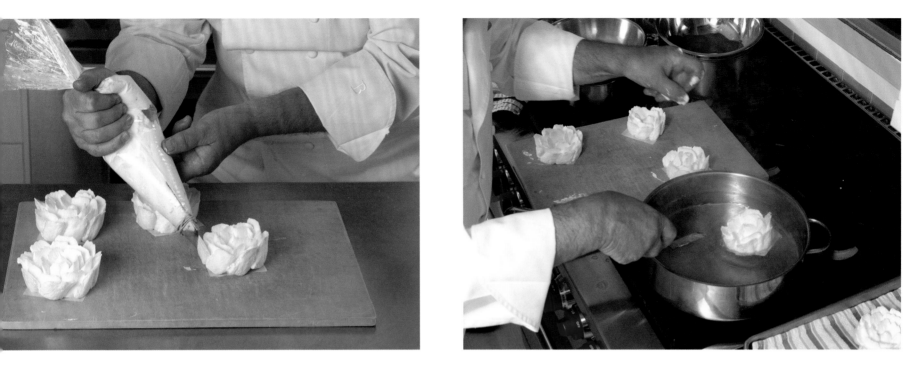

Place each piece of parchment paper on the simmering water and let the rose slide off.

The roses may be presented on a platter of raspberry sauce, garnished with fresh raspberries.

This snowman and miniature gingerbread house was an individually plated dessert, served on the Reagan China for a family and friends holiday event. The dacquoise meringue was cut to form the base under the house. The snowman was formed with small scoops of pear sorbet stacked together. The bottom scoop of sorbet was hollowed out and filled with orange parfait.

DACQUOISE MERINGUE

1 cup almond flour
1½ cups granulated sugar
2 tablespoons all-purpose flour
5 tablespoons whole milk
8 large egg whites
Confectioners' sugar

Preheat oven to 350 degrees

1. Line two sheet pans (12 x 18") with parchment paper.
2. In a large bowl, combine the almond flour, ½ cup of the sugar, and the flour. Stir in the milk to make a soft paste, like choux paste or mashed potatoes.
3. Place the egg whites in the bowl of an electric mixer fitted with the whisk attachment, and whip on high speed until soft peaks form. With the mixer running on high, slowly and steadily run the sugar into the whites. Continue whipping until a meringue forms. It will be shiny and hold firm peaks.
4. Fold half of the meringue into the almond mixture. Fold in the remaining meringue. Make sure not to overfold the meringue and deflate it.
5. Using a no. 8 plain round piping tip (about ¾ inch), pipe the meringue to fill the sheet pans. It may not fill both pans. Dust with confectioners' sugar.
6. Place the sheet pans in the preheated ovens. Prop the oven door open with a small ball of aluminum foil to allow moisture to escape. Bake the meringues for 20 minutes.

Reduce temperature to 300 degrees

7. Bake for another 40 minutes until the meringues are firm and golden brown.
8. Remove the pans from the oven. Slide the meringues, still on the parchment paper, off the hot pans and let cool. Use the meringues immediately, or wrap in plastic and keep at room temperature for a week.

MERINGUE MUSHROOMS

8 large egg whites
2 cups granulated sugar
2 cups confectioners' sugar
3 tablespoons all-purpose flour
Cocoa powder for dusting

Preheat oven to 250 degrees

1. Place the egg whites in the bowl of an electric mixer fitted with the whisk attachment, and whip on high speed until soft peaks form. With the mixer running on high, slowly and steadily run the sugar into the whites. Continue whipping until a meringue forms. It will be shiny and hold firm peaks.

2. Sift together confectioners' sugar and flour and fold into meringue.

3. Put the meringue in a pastry bag fitted with a no. 6 round tube.

4. On a half sheet pan lined with parchment, pipe mushroom stems in a shape similar to chocolate kisses. Place in the oven, with door propped open with a small ball of aluminum foil to allow moisture to escape. Bake for about 1 hour until stems are dry. Remove the pan from the oven and leave the dried stems attached to the parchment paper.

5. Line a sheet pan with a very damp towel and top it with parchment paper. You may have to use some of the meringue to glue it down.

6. Pipe mushroom caps on the parchment. Dust the caps with cocoa powder using a very fine sieve.

7. Place the pan in the oven. As soon as the caps are solid to the touch (they will still be soft on the inside) remove the pan. Carefully lift each cap and place it on one of the dry stems.

Reduce temperature to 180 degrees

8. Return the pan of assembled mushrooms to the oven and let them dry fully, for about 1 to 1½ hours.

These versatile meringue mushrooms can be served alone or paired with many desserts, including buche de Noel, frangipan, or orange parfait.

Mascarpone Mousse

The mascarpone mouse is a dessert in itself, but it may also be paired with other desserts.

Spice cake (*see recipe page 166*)
2 cups heavy cream, chilled
4 large egg whites
1 cup sugar
⅓ cup water
8 ounces white chocolate
3 tablespoons cold water
1½ envelopes unflavored gelatin (or 9 sheets)
1 pound mascarpone, room temperature
¼ cup Grand Marnier, or other orange-flavored liqueur

1. Place the heavy cream in a clean bowl of an electric mixer fitted with the whisk attachment, and whip until it holds a soft peak.
2. Place the egg whites in a second clean bowl of an electric mixer fitted with the whisk attachment. Combine the sugar and water in a saucepan and without stirring, cook the mixture until it reaches a soft boil.
3. On high speed beat egg whites while dribbling the sugar syrup in to the bowl. Decrease the speed to medium and continue to whip until the egg whites reach firm peaks and are cool.
4. Put 1 inch of water in a saucepan and place on very low heat. Place chocolate in bowl and place over, but not touching, the warm water. Stir until the chocolate is fully melted. Remove the bowl from the heat and let it cool until just slightly warm.
5. Put 1 inch of water into a saucepan and bring barely to a simmer. Put 3 tablespoons of water in a small bowl. Sprinkle gelatin into the water in the bowls for about 5 minutes until absorbed. Place gelatin bowl over heated water in the sauce pan for about 30 seconds or until gelatin is completely dissolved.
6. In a separate bowl, quickly whisk the melted gelatin with mascarpone. Then mix in the Grand Marnier and the melted white chocolate. Quickly fold in meringue and whipped cream.
7. Pour mousse into a 4-cup mold, cover and refrigerate for at least 6 hours and up to two days.

Chestnut Mousse

3 cups heavy cream, chilled
2 cups sweet chestnut spread (*available in specialty stores*)

1. Put heavy cream in the bowl an electric mixer fitted with the whisk the attachment and whip until it becomes soft.
2. Gently fold the heavy cream into the chestnut spread.
3. Using a pastry bag fitted with a no. 8 start tip, pipe mousse rosettes directly onto the dessert plates.

This plated dessert included a small piece of three-layered chocolate cake with a whipped ganache filling wrapped as a present with a shiny, dark chocolate glaze and decorated with a buttercream rose. The golden ribbon was made of rolled marzipan. Near the present is a piped rosette of chestnut mousse. The chocolate tree is decorated with royal icing garlands and ornaments and topped with a marzipan star. The plate was finished with a raspberry sauce and raspberries dusted with powdered sugar.

The White House has a collection of fine tableware, and one of my favorite services was the red-bordered Reagan china (seen here). Over the years, I was permitted to use rare pieces from earlier historic services on special occasions. After the event, I personally hand washed the china and saw to its safe return to storage.

Passion Fruit Mousse

Spice cake (*see recipe page 166*)
1 cup heavy cream, chilled
4 large egg whites
3 tablespoons cold water
1 envelope unflavored gelatin (or 6 sheets)
1 cup sugar
1 cup frozen passion fruit puree, thawed

1. Place the heavy cream in a chilled bowl of an electric mixer fitted with the whisk attachment and whip until it holds a soft peak.

2. Place the egg whites in a separate bowl of the mixer, and whip until they reach a soft peak. With the mixer on high speed, slowly add the sugar and mix until the meringue is fully formed and holds a firm peak.

3. Put 1 inch of water in a sauce pan and bring to a simmer. Place the 3 tablespoons of water in a small bowl and sprinkle in gelatin. Leave the gelatin for about 5 minutes to fully absorb the water. Place the gelatin over the simmering water for about 30 seconds and stir until it fully dissolves.

4. Stir sugar into the passion fruit puree. Quickly whisk in the melted gelatin by hand. Fold meringue and the whipped cream into the passion fruit puree.

5. Spread on top of spice cake and then chill.

PORT WINE MOUSSE

6 large egg yolks

½ cup plus 2 tablespoons granulated sugar

½ cup good Port wine

½ envelope of granulated unflavored gelatin (or 3 sheets)

¾ cup heavy cream (with no sugar)

3 large egg whites

GARNISH

Fresh figs, thinly sliced

Fresh raspberries

1. Prepare a 6-cup soufflé mold fitted with a parchment or plastic collar that goes 1 to 1½ inches above the top rim of the mold.

2. Combine yolks, ½ cup sugar, and Port wine in a metal bowl. Place the bowl over a saucepan of simmering water. Whisk the mixture by hand, 8 to 10 minutes, until mixture is thick and creamy and has expanded in volume.

3. In a small bowl, soften gelatin in 2 tablespoons of water and then place bowl over warm water to melt. Stir the melted gelatin into the yolk mixture and allow to cool to room temperature.

4. In the bowl of an electric mixer fitted with the whisk attachment, beat the heavy cream to firm peaks.

5. In a separate bowl, whip the egg whites to a soft peak using the electric mixer. Then add 2 tablespoons granulated sugar and beat until firm peaks form.

6. Whip the heavy cream until soft peaks form. Simultaneously fold the whipped cream and meringue into the Port wine mixture.

7. Place the Port wine mousse into the prepared soufflé mold and chill for several hours.

8. Cover the exposed surface of the mousse with thin slices of fresh figs and present with a stack of fresh raspberries in the center of the top.

9. Remove the collar just before serving.

This dessert should be considered a frozen soufflé, and is very refreshing after the main course. The Port wine mousse is frozen in a traditional soufflé mold. The plastic collar helps mold the mousse high above the rim, as if it were a hot soufflé coming out of the oven. The dessert was normally served with a large bowl of raspberry sauce and a tray of assorted cookies.

WHITE HOUSE HOLIDAY RECIPES

FRANGIPANE

At the White House we used frangipane to create petit fours for the holiday buffet trays. Almond flour may be substituted with hazelnut or pistachio flour.

1 cup (2 sticks) unsalted butter, softened

1 cup granulated sugar

2 cups almond flour

5 large eggs, room temperature

½ tablespoon pure vanilla extract

1 teaspoon grated lemon zest

¼ cup plus ½ tablespoon all-purpose flour

2 tablespoons dark rum (optional)

Preheat oven to 350 degrees

1. Place the butter, sugar, and almond flour in the bowl of an electric mixer fitted with the paddle attachment and whip on medium speed until fully blended.

2. Add the eggs, one at a time and scrape down the bowl after each addition.

3. Stir in the vanilla, lemon zest, rum, and all-purpose flour and mix until just combined.

4. Spread to a depth of one inch in a sheet pan lined with parchment paper and bake for 12 to 15 minutes until light brown and firm.

5. Serve like cake or use small cookie cutters to make bite-sized shapes for use in petit fours.

ORANGE PARFAIT

4 large egg yolks
1½ teaspoons finely grated orange zest
½ cup heavy syrup *(recipe below)*
1½ cups heavy cream
¼ cup Grand Marnier

Preheat oven to 350 degrees

1. Place the egg yolks in the bowl of an electric mixer fitted with the whisk attachment.
2. Put the heavy syrup in a small sauce pan and bring to a boil. On high speed slowly pour the hot syrup into the bowl with the egg yolk. Be careful not to pour any sugar on the whisk. Reduce to medium speed and mix for several minutes, until the mixture is cool, pale yellow, and increased in volume.
3. Place the cream into the bowl of an electric mixer fitted with the whisk attachment, and whip to soft peaks.
4. Gently fold the heavy cream and Grand Marnier into the yolk mixture.
5. Place in mold and freeze. May be served with fresh fruit.

HEAVY SYRUP

1 cup water
1 cup granulated sugar
1 tablespoon light corn syrup

Mix the ingredients together and bring to a boil.

Chartreuse Ice Cream

You will need an ice cream maker for this recipe.

1 quart whole milk
10 large egg yolks
¾ cup granulated sugar
½ cup Chartreuse, or to taste
¼ cup cold heavy cream

1. Place the milk in a saucepan and bring to a soft boil.
2. Whisk together the yolks and granulated sugar. While whisking, slowly pour in half of the hot milk. Continue stirring until all of the sugar is dissolved. Pour the yolk mixture into the saucepan and combine with the hot milk. Lower the heat and cook until the mixture coats the back of a wooden spoon and reaches about 180 degrees.
3. Pass the custard through a fine sieve and stir over ice to cool.
4. Stir in the Chartreuse and chill in the refrigerator for 4 hours or overnight.
5. Stir in the heavy cream. Put mixture in an ice cream machine and freeze for about 20 minutes.
6. Shape the ice cream and place in the freezer to cure for 2 hours.

Pomegranate Sorbet

You will need an ice cream maker for this recipe.

2 cups fresh pomegranate juice
¾ cup sugar
1 tablespoon fresh lemon juice
½ envelope granulated gelatin (or 3 sheets of gelatin)

1. Prepare the fresh pomegranate juice and chill in the refrigerator.
2. Stir in sugar and make sure it is dissolved, then add the lemon juice.
3. Soften the gelatin in a small bowl with 2 tablespoons of water and melt over warm water. Stir gelatin into pomegranate juice.
4. Place pomegranate sorbet in an ice cream machine and freeze for about 20 minutes.
5. Shape the sorbet and put in the freezer to cure for 2 hours.

The Christmas tree in this White House dessert was made of Chartreuse ice cream. The branches are made from ice cream piped onto ice cream frozen into a triangular tree shape. The tree was decorated with fresh berries and marzipan stars and bows. An angel molded of white chocolate was placed on top of the tree. The tree was presented standing on an oval of dried meringue. The pinecones were made of pomegranate sorbet quenelle. The scales of the pinecones were made in a mold with tempered chocolate. Once the chocolate set it was released from the mold, and the scales were pushed into the pomegranate sorbet. The whole cone was then sprayed with thinned couverture chocolate.

POACHED STRAWBERRIES

3 pounds (10 cups) whole strawberries,
cleaned, stems removed

2½ cups plus one cup granulated sugar

½ cup water

1½ tablespoons apple pectin

A few drops of red food coloring

2 cups Devonshire cream (optional)

2 cups of lemon cream (optional)

1. Combine the strawberries, 2½ cups of granulated sugar, and water in a large pot and stir to combine. Place the pot on high heat until the sugar melts, and continue cooking until the berries are soft.
2. Remove three-fourths of the juice in the pot and reserve for another use.
3. Combine 1 cup of granulated sugar with the apple pectin and stir into the berries still in the pot.
4. Add 3 to 4 drops of red food coloring and cook 5 to 8 minutes. Pour the berries and juice into a dish and allow them to cool in a single layer.
5. Store in the refrigerator until ready to use in desserts.
6. If serving with cream, fold the Devonshire cream into the lemon cream.

LEMON CREAM

5 large lemons

1½ cups granulated sugar

4 large egg

1½ cup (2 sticks) unsalted butter, cut into cubes

1. Remove the zest from the lemons with a grater, and set it aside. Cut each lemon in half and squeeze the juice into a small bowl.
2. Combine the zest, juice, sugar, eggs, butter in a heavy-bottomed sauce pan, and bring to a boil over medium high heat.
3. Boil for 30 seconds, whisking constantly, and make sure the mixture is not sticking to the bottom of the pan.
4. Remove the pan from the heat and pour the mixture through a fine-mesh strainer into a non-reactive bowl. Cool to room temperature. Refrigerate in an airtight container for up to one week, or freeze for up to two months.

For a special dessert, which we first made for Prime Minister Tony Blair, we placed poached strawberries in a molded chocolate bucket decorated with green piping. We made a thin roulade biscuit and covered it with raspberry jam. The roulade was rolled tightly into a 1 1/2 inch cylinder then chilled and cut into 1/8 inch slices. These were placed edge-to-edge on the base and inside of the bucket. The bucket was filled with alternating layers of the whole poached strawberries and a lemon cream lightened with Devonshire cream. The top layer of strawberries was decorated with small leaves piped in green buttercream.

WHITE HOUSE HOLIDAY RECIPES

Fresh Fruit Salad

2 to 3 medium oranges, peeled, and in segments

⅓ ripe pineapple, peeled and cored

Grapes, peeled and seeded

Strawberries

Bananas

Ripe pears

Plums, pitted

Kiwi

Any seasonal fruit of your choice

Fresh pomegranate seeds (optional)

Apple juice

Liquor to taste (optional)

Heavy syrup, to taste (*see page 190*)

1. Prepare all of the fruit by peeling and pitting where appropriate and cut into uniform size pieces.
2. Combine the fruit in a large bowl and stir in sugar to taste.
3. Pour in enough apple juice to cover all of the fruit. The apple juice will preserve the colors of the fruits and contribute a nice flavor to the salad.
4. Store the fruit salad in the refrigerator. A bag of ice can be placed on top of the fruit salad to chill faster.
5. Pour off the apple juice and add the heavy syrup and liquor to taste.

Glossary of Pastry Terms

EQUIPMENT

bundt pan a circular tube pan with a fluted pattern on the sides and bottom, used for dense pound cake recipes

docker any pointed tool used to prick holes in rolled dough to allow steam to escape during baking; it is essential to dock gingerbread dough so that the sheets will bake flat

french bread mold a metal mold used for holding the shape of a French baguette during baking; it can also be used to shape pastries and for features on gingerbread projects

paper cone a tool used to hold and pipe icing; it is made by rolling a triangle of paper (often parchment paper) and clipping off the bottom tip (also called a cornet)

parchment paper a paper used to line baking pans that eliminates the need to treat the pan with shortening or butter and flour

piping tubes used with a piping bag to decorate pastries; large tubes comes in four basic shapes (plain round, open star, closed star, and French star), and each shape comes in 10 sizes (0–9)

sheet pan a rectangular metal pan with low side walls used for baking sheet cakes; the most common sizes are the full sheet pan (18 x 24"), half sheet pan (12 x 18"), quarter sheet pan (9 x 13"), and eighth sheet pan (6 x 10")

stencil a pattern often cut into a thin piece of paper used for backing and for tracing designs out of melted chocolate or soft cookie batter

INGREDIENTS AND COMPONENTS

almond paste a mixture of ground almonds, sugar, and egg whites used to flavor cakes and cookies

beurre manié a thickening agent made from an equal combination of butter and all-purpose flour

bread flour a high protein flour used to make bread products leavened with yeast

buttercream an icing in its most basic form made with butter blended with confectioners' sugar or sugar syrup

buttermilk the liquid remaining after the cream is removed from milk to make butter; when treated with an acid it is called cultured buttermilk

cake flour a low protein flour used to make tender pastries

caramel sugar cooked to a dark, syrupy consistency used to flavor desserts

cardamom a pungent spice used frequently in Indian cuisines

Chartreuse a distilled liqueur infused with a secret combination of herbs, known only to Carthusian monks

choux paste a French paste made of milk, butter, flour, and eggs; the paste is first cooked on the stove and then shaped and baked in the oven, where steam creates hollow shapes

clover honey a light colored honey made from clover blossoms

Cointreau an orange-flavored French liqueur

confectioners' sugar finely powdered granulated sugar (also called powdered sugar or 10X sugar)

crème anglaise French for "English cream," a light pouring custard used as a dessert sauce; it is a mixture of sugar, egg yolks, hot milk, and vanilla

couverture chocolate chocolate with a minimum of 31 percent cocoa butter that is used to create hard, shiny coatings on pastries

dacquoise a light, crisp meringue made with ground nuts, often layered with buttercream

Devonshire cream a rich imported English cream with an acidic taste

fondant, rolled a paste made of confectioners' sugar, glucose, and gelatin; it is rolled out flat and used to decorate pastries; in gingerbread projects, it is especially useful for creating flat details such as windows and doors

ganache a mixture of chocolate and heavy cream; it is used as a center for truffles, cake filling, and pastry glaze

gelatin a substance with a jelly-like consistency when cooled, used to thicken and stabilize liquids such as pastry cream and crème anglaise; available in granulated and sheet form

Grand Marnier a French liqueur that contains brandy and oranges

hazelnut flour a flour that contains finely ground hazelnuts

jimmies tiny chocolate pieces similar to sprinkles that are used to decorate desserts

Kirsch a clear, colorless fruit brandy usually made from double distilling cherries

lemon oil oil extracted from lemon rinds

marzipan a combination of almond paste, sugar, and corn syrup, used as an icing, for decorative work, or for molding candies and figures

mascarpone a soft double or triple cream cow's milk cheese

meringue powder a fine white powder made of dried egg whites and cornstarch that becomes a fluffy meringue when water is added and beaten at a high speed

passion fruit a small, round tropical fruit with wrinkled purple skin and edible seeds

pastillage a modeling paste made of sugar and gelatin used for decorative work such as flowers or architectural details

pastry cream a rich custard of eggs and sugar thickened with flour or cornstarch, used as a filling for cakes and pastries

pâte sucrée a sweet, tender dough that can be rolled and cut to form cookies or tart shells

pectin a food thickener used in jams and jellies

pomegranate a medium-sized tart fruit with pink flesh that contains many seeds

Port wine a fortified, dark red wine from Portugal

royal icing an icing made of confectioners' sugar and egg whites, used to decorate pastries and create fine details on gingerbread houses

sprinkles small colored sugar pieces used as decoration on desserts

tempered chocolate couverture chocolate melted to the appropriate condition, consistency, and temperature for dipping or coating chocolate and pastries; sets quickly and has a hard, shiny surface; used as a "glue" when constructing gingerbread houses and as a backing for gingerbread sheets

TECHNIQUES

blown sugar pulled hard-crack sugar that is made into thin-walled, hollow shapes by being blown up like a balloon

candied cooked in a sugar syrup to give it a sweet, glossy coating

clarified butter what remains after the water and the milk solids have been removed from butter

crystallizing the process of forming crystals in sugar and cocoa butter

docking the technique of pricking small holes in rolled dough before baking to keep the dough from blistering or warping

egg wash a mixture of egg yolks and cream brushed on dough before baking to create a shiny brown surface; the more fat in the egg wash, the darker the resulting color

firm peak a condition when egg whites or heavy cream has been whipped until it is stiff

floodwork a technique that runs thin royal icing or chocolate into a pre-piped design (also known as run outs or transfer)

footing a hard chocolate base added to the bottom of a pastry by dipping it in tempered chocolate; the footing prevents the bottom of pastries from sticking to the serving dish and adds a decorative effect

glazing a thin, shiny liquid coat applied over a cake or pastry

hard-crack sugar sugar mixed with water and glucose and heated to 300 to 310 degrees; used to make blown- and pulled-sugar decorations

meringue whipped egg whites

piping forcing icing or chocolate through a pastry bag equipped with a tube to decorate pastries

pulled sugar sugar that is boiled to the hard-crack stage, allowed to harden, and then pulled or stretched until it develops a pearly sheen

soft peak a condition when egg whites or heavy cream has been mixed until it barely stands up on its own

thread stage stage when sugar and water are heated to approximately 223 to 234 degrees and the syrup drips from a spoon on threads

TYPES OF DESSERTS

biscuit a French cake or pastry consisting of eggs, sugar, flour, and whipped cream; roulade and lady finger desserts are both considered biscuits

buche de Noel a traditional French Christmas cake made with a roulade, filled and rolled into the shape of a log, and trimmed with edible holiday decorations.

génoise a light sponge cake made with eggs, sugar, flour, and sometimes melted butter

meringue, French a baked meringue made of granulated sugar added to whipped egg whites; this is the method best known to home cooks

petit four a small cake cut from a pound or sponge cake and frosted, often layered and decorated, designed as an individual dessert to be eaten in one or two bites; *glace*—small cakes and tarts glazed with fondant icing; *frais*—bite-size versions of fresh pastries such as a fruit tart or an éclair; and *prestige*—pastries composed of many components and decorations

quenelle a dumpling consisting of a mixture of creamed fish or meat combined with breadcrumbs and an egg binding and poached; also refers to an egg shape

roulade a biscuit sponge cake baked in a thin sheet, filled with a cream, and rolled

sabayon a foamy cake or sauce made of egg yolks whipped with wine or liqueur, served over fruit

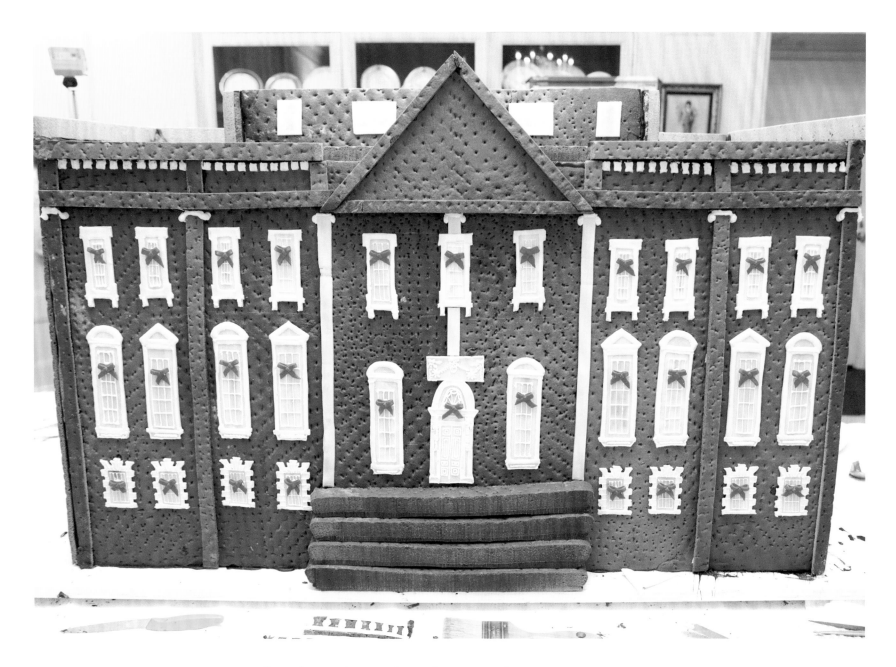

The White House Gingerbread template provided in the pocket on the back inside cover of this book is designed for creating a house similar to the Red and White Gingerbread House, which I made in 2006, but on a smaller scale that can be done in the home kitchen.

INDEX

Numbers in brackets indicate illustrations.

Eileen Cortese photographs work in progress during the construction of the 2006 Red & White Gingerbread House.

ILLUSTRATION CREDITS

All images are in the collection of
Roland Mesnier unless listed below.

ACKNOWLEDGMENTS

This book was made possible through the help and encouragement of many colleagues and professionals, my friends new and old, and the many devoted readers who encouraged me to continue to share my stories and recipes with this new title.

My list of thanks begins with Stewart D. McLaurin, president of the White House Historical Association, who enthusiastically supported this publication from its beginning. Marcia Anderson and her staff in the Publications Department transformed the concept for this book into a reality. Lauren Zook, production manager, coordinated many details and assisted with the design. Fiona Griffin, the editorial director, Rhonda Murchison, editorial specialist, and Ann Hofstra Grogg, consulting editor, ensured that the text was accurate and carefully edited.

The White House is a special place and I was privileged to serve five first families. I owe a special debt of gratitude to first ladies Rosalynn Carter, Nancy Reagan, Barbara Bush, Hillary Clinton, and Laura Bush, who each taught and inspired me by sharing their family Christmas traditions and entertaining experience and by allowing me creative freedom. The staff of the Richard Nixon, Gerald R. Ford, Jimmy Carter, Ronald Reagan, George Bush, William J. Clinton, and George W. Bush presidential libraries made many photographs available. Melissa Montgomery, special assistant to Rosalynn Carter, and Audrey Akers from the office of Laura Bush, facilitated our correspondence.

The Operations crew professionally moved the showpiece into the State Dining Room every year without accident.

Thanks also go to my colleagues and friends at the White House beginning with Gary Walters, the Chief Usher from 1986 to 2007, and the staff of the Office of the Curator who gave me their support during my years as executive pastry chef, especially during the holiday season. For more than twenty years, Betty Monkman, former curator of the White House, provided scholarly advice on matters related to the history of the White House and its collection. More recently William Allman, the present curator, and Lydia Tederick, assistant curator, and their colleagues Melissa Naulin, Donna Hayashi Smith, and Jill DeWitt, advised on the historical content and photographs in this book.

The construction of the gingerbread showpiece each year was an enormous task and could not have been possible without the help of the other professional staff at the White House. My former assistant Susie Morrison, now the executive pastry chef, was instrumental in the success of our ambitious Christmas projects. The talented pastry assistants who helped bake enormous amounts of cookies and desserts each holiday season and Marlene Roudebush, whose marzipan creations added unique details to the gingerbread houses and whose personal photographs of the gingerbread houses, marzipan, and holiday desserts were loaned to help illustrate this book. The holiday cookies and desserts were always made with the best ingredients from around the world even during the busiest time of the year, thanks to the Storeroom staff.

The construction of the gingerbread showpiece could not have been possible without the help of the other professional staff at the White House.

Many departments deserve my thanks for generously sharing their specialized expertise: the Carpenter Shop and the Paint Shop built custom bases strong enough to support the weight of the gingerbread houses; the Electric Shop, created intricate wiring to illuminate the houses; the Operations crew, professionally moved the showpiece into the State Dining Room every year without accident and took their work very seriously.

Our talented photographer Bruce White captured the stunning new images of cookies and desserts that are featured in the recipes portion of this book. Lydia Schlosser granted the use of her wonderful kitchen facilities for the photo shoot as well as her baking services when recreating the recipes. Lucinda Seale, cookbook author, read the manuscript and gave valuable advice for improvements. James Brooks, Debbie Buckey, and David Blysma at Peake-Delancey assisted with prepress and Nancy Freeman and the staff at Verona Libri ensured the highest quality printing.

My professional colleagues Chef Patrick O'Connell, owner of the Inn at Little Washington in Virginia, Chef Thomas Keller of French Laundry in California, and Chef Daniel Boulud owner of award-winning restaurants in New York all kindly offered their encouragement.